ARISE AND SHINE EKKLESIA

Make Your Home a Place
Where People Meet Jesus

DR. WILLIE JOUBERT

Tellwell Talent
www.tellwell.ca

ISBN
978-0-2288-5459-3 (Hardcover)
978-0-2288-5458-6 (Paperback)
978-0-2288-5460-9 (eBook)

Table of Contents

ACKNOWLEDGEMENTS

This book is intended as a guide for those who have heard the Spirit's call to walk through the gates of control out of the Levitical structures of the Western Church. I am deeply indebted to the pioneering remnant that joined with us to meet in local homes and be the church and thus showed that the New Testament model can function within our modern society.

A Special thanks to the following:

- Roger and Ginette and the church at your home
- Lawrence and Sharon and the church at your home
- Kim and Sandra and the young people at your homes
- My wife Eda and the church at our house

I also want to express my sincere thanks for Jerry and Wilma for your encouragement and input together with those who met at your home in the beginning.

A very special thank you again to Ron Fair in Finland for the encouragement and input from abroad and the regular notes from the churches in Finland, Brazil and India that you have sent me through the past year.

Also, a special word of thanks to Gary Meehan for the original cover design when we hand copied and distributed this booklet in the beginning. We treasure the friendship and support.

I thank you, Rodger and Mary, Martin and Kim, Peter, Jan and Kathy and Paul and Suzette for your financial support to help with the publication of this series.

Above all, I wish to thank our Lord Jesus. You have been faithful and true and never fail to drop in and meet with us when we open the door to visit with friends. Through Your Spirit you have made it so easy to experience your presence filling ordinary homes with your glory. You are indeed the same – yesterday, today and forever – for you meet us every time just like you did with so many, as recorded in the Gospels. We witness your presence changing ordinary people into extraordinary royal priests!

INTRODUCTION

As we entered into this new Millennium there is a growing awareness that the Church of Christ is in the process of major change. The Ekklesia is rising up as spoken forth in the prophetic word of Isaiah 60:1-3:

> *Arise, shine, for your light has come,*
> *and the glory of the LORD rises upon you.*
> *See, darkness covers the earth*
> *and thick darkness is over the peoples, but*
> *the LORD rises upon you*
> *and his glory appears over you.*
> *Nations will come to your light,*
> *and kings to the brightness of your dawn.*

As this is beginning to happen it is very clear that the current structures of the church will not be able to handle these changes. The foundations of the Western Church need to be restored and no amount of patching will fill the cracks as I wrote in "Restoring the broken foundations." There is a growing awareness that the Levitical order of the priesthood, which was re-introduced into the Church when Constantine was converted in the fourth century, needs to be totally rejected, for in Christ this old order was replaced by the order of Melchizedek. The latter implies that every believer is a priest and called and anointed for full-time ministry wherever the believer may be at any time. As the Ekklesia or Third Day Church[1] arises, the truth of the priesthood of the believer will be central and the current structures of the Church will be shattered by the rising up of ordinary people to fulfill the call on their lives, as I wrote in "Ordinary people, extraordinary royal priests." This new wine will tear the old wineskins and

---

[1] There is a growing trend to refer to the church as Ekklesia from the Greek. The background is that more and more believers begin to realize that the church does not really reflect what Jesus had in mind when he spoke about it in Matthew 16:18-19. The term 'Third Day Church' is a reference to the prophetic nature of Jesus' words when confronted with the threat from King Herod recorded in Luke 13:32: "Go tell that fox, I will drive out demons and heal people today and tomorrow, and on the third day I will be perfected. I must keep going today and tomorrow and the next day – for surely no prophet can die outside Jerusalem." The reference is first to his death on the cross and the resurrection on the third day, but prophetically it speaks of the church entering the third millennium and being perfected as his body, for one day is as a thousand years with the Lord (2 Peter 3:8). This is not the place to discuss the issues, but I mention it in case someone wonders about the terminology. Whatever term we choose, the reality is that the church of the future will need to change and in my opinion the change will require that we return to the simplicity and power of the church in the New Testament and shed much of the historical baggage we accumulated through the ages – and it is far more than changing our terminology.

Jesus warned us about this when he said the following recorded in Matthew 9:16-17:

> *No one sews a patch of unshrunk cloth on an old garment, for the patch will pull away from the garment, making the tear worse. Neither do men pour new wine into old wineskins. If they do, the skins will burst, the wine will run out and the wineskins will be ruined. No, they pour new wine into new wineskins, and both are preserved.*

The Church, as we know it in the Western world will not last in its present form. The rising tide of the Spirit moving in and through ordinary people in increasing ways, is calling us to walk in the way that the early believers walked. They were known as "the people of The Way." In this Third Day Jesus is perfecting his body as he prophetically said when he was warned that Herod wanted to kill him, Luke 13:32:

> *And he said unto them, "Go ye, and tell that fox, Behold, I cast out devils, and I do cures today and tomorrow, and the third day I shall be perfected."* KJV

Thus, we are called in this Third Day to walk in 'Radical Authenticity,' as I wrote in the book with that title. Our Lord is calling out a remnant, willing to walk away from the current confining structures and become radically authentic by putting faith into action. As this happens, the Third Day Church will rise up and the glory of the Lord will begin to become visible in ways and in places where it was hidden before. One of the keys to this is that ordinary homes will be opened, as believers recognize that they are called to be the Church rather than to go to a building called a church. Ordinary homes will once again be the preferred place of meeting for believers as it was in the vibrant early years of the Church and the best wine, aged for 2000 years, will be served by ordinary people walking in their anointing, as the servant leaders equip and release them to become all they can be in Christ. Resources that are being wasted in maintaining underused buildings to run ineffective programs developed and led by Levitical priests will become available for effective Kingdom ministry, as it was when the Church began 2000 years ago. Lives of people will be changed as the power of the Spirit is being released, often through what seems to be the most unlikely people – the simple and unlearned, who walk in childlike faith.

In the books mentioned above, I shared the foundational issues about these changes and how God challenged and moved us from the comfort of the four walls of the Church and the security it offered, to this walk of radical authenticity. In the process, we witnessed the power of God to transform lives when ordinary people open their homes and simply begin to walk in obedience to the call of Christ upon their lives. **This book is intended to be a practical guide for those who have heard the Spirit and are willing to walk in radical authenticity. It is specifically intended to share practical insights that will help those who want to make their homes places**

where Jesus meets with people and where his glory is manifested and the power of the Spirit is released in the presence of his people. I believe that the prophetic promise spoken by Haggai about the rebuilding of the temple, is a word that is being spoken forth anew today, as Jesus is restoring his Church in this Third Day: Haggai 2:6-9:

> *"This is what the LORD Almighty says: 'In a little while I will once more shake the heavens and the earth, the sea and the dry land. I will shake all nations, and the desired of all nations will come, and I will fill this house with glory,' says the LORD Almighty.*
>
> *'The silver is mine and the gold is mine,' declares the LORD Almighty. 'The glory of this present house will be greater than the glory of the former house,' says the LORD Almighty. 'And in this place I will grant peace,' declares the LORD Almighty."*

This is a day of small beginnings for the house church movement in the West, but not to be despised, as is written in Zechariah 4:6-10:

> *So, the angel said to me, "This is the word of the LORD to Zerubbabel: 'Not by might nor by power, but by my Spirit,' says the LORD Almighty.*

What are you, O mighty mountain? Before Zerubbabel you will become level ground. Then he will bring out the capstone to shouts of `God bless it! God bless it!'"

Then the word of the LORD came to me: "The hands of Zerubbabel have laid the foundation of this temple; his hands will also complete it. Then you will know that the LORD Almighty has sent me to you.

Who despises the day of small things? Men will rejoice when they see the plumb line in the hand of Zerubbabel."

Your home and the first meetings may seem small and insignificant, but do not despise the day of small beginnings. This movement is of the Spirit and it will not be stopped or derailed. It is not just a way to the future, but it is The Way. Your home is not just a place where people will meet for a season and then to move on to a "real church building." This is the point where we need to begin to understand the rising up of this Third Day Church.

The Church In Your House

It is a very simple issue but of vital importance as we look at the Third Day Church rising up. **The Church meeting in the home is the church – period! I repeat: The Church meeting in my house is the church and nothing less than the Church!** It sounds ridiculous to have to say this, but it is the single most important issue that we face as we move into this new paradigm. For many this issue is the one that will make or break their response to the call of Jesus to walk in radical authenticity. We face the fact that the Western mindset sees the Church as a building where believers gather on a Sunday at the appointed time and that the home may be used for meetings, but this use is not "Church."

We have found it absolutely essential to deal with this mindset up front. It has to be settled – and not just with a rational consent. It has to be settled in your heart. You need to be at peace knowing in your heart that when you meet with others in a house setting, it is Church. Jesus said that where two or three are gathered in his name, he would be there. He really meant that and he does show up. He is not less there than in a building called a church. The Holy Spirit is not less able to meet needs when we meet with a few others in a home setting. The prayers are not less effective when an ordinary brother or sister prays for someone at the house, than when "the pastor" prays at "the church."

As we read this, it is not difficult to understand and agree. However, those who grew up with the Western mindset have been indoctrinated and programmed to think of church as being a meeting in a "church building" with the programs and Levitical systems of worship and leadership. This has been part and parcel of the Western mindset for centuries! We talk about going to church, rather than being the church. Moreover, going to church is very specifically tied to Sunday mornings as being the special time to have church. For some it helps the transition if the home church meetings are on the Sunday morning and we know of home churches directed by the Lord to meet at that time. However, the meetings do not have to be on a Sunday at all. Those accustomed to meet in a church on Sunday mornings and who respond to the call of becoming part of the remnant to re-lay the broken foundations, once they step out, immediately face the pressure from religious spirits to "get to church" on Sunday morning! It can be a feeling of unease inside oneself or come from church members in a traditional setting, asking where you go to church now. No matter how you analyze this, if you seek the Spirit you will find it has no roots in Scripture, but rather springs from the manipulation through guilt having been taught that you "have to attend the church that meets in the building." After all, only those who were not fully committed stayed away from church on Sunday. (Please note that this is not a license to ignore regular meetings with believers, which are very much Scriptural, but we are talking about the pressure of the traditional understanding of the Church).

As we look at this, it is further good to note that as you meet in the home, it does not have to become church, as most Westerners are accustomed to. We will deal with the structure of the meeting later, but it is very important to recognize that it is not simply making the house to be a smaller replica of "the church". Thus, it is not about having a Levitical model of church in the home, particularly not having a "pastor" to do the ministry!

The first step in establishing a home church is the willingness to open your home to be a place where Jesus can meet with you and those that come. In doing that, you need to know in your heart that that is what church is all about and that when you meet together, that is being the Church. Allow the Spirit to write the truth about being the Church in your heart. Deal with the misconceptions and religious baggage and settle the issue about your house being the primary place where you meet as church until you have peace in your innermost being. It is good to read the Scriptures for yourself and note how often we read about "the church that meets in someone's house." If necessary, check for yourself and verify that nowhere in Scripture do we read that it is "the committee" or "the cell group" that meets in the home.

In saying these things, there is another reason why we need to settle the issue deep down up front. Many start in the home as home church, but as this grows, there is pressure to abandon the house and find "a suitable location for the church." In fact, the traditional model of church planting in North America uses the home as a base from which to launch a church plant. When the house church is properly established and functioning, the enemy will be very active in trying to convince you that the way forward is to revert to the traditional Levitical model and that the leader is to be the "anointed pastor or apostle." Thus, it is very important to know the Scriptures and to understand and follow the church model that functioned in the first centuries following the death and resurrection of our Lord. I have written about this in the other books and do not want to repeat these foundational issues here again, but it is imperative to know how the early church functioned and to compare the fruit of that tree to the lack of fruit of the Western model. In that way we will not fail and we will know why we do not want to follow the Levitical model in which most of us have been raised.

With that being established, it is time to open the door and to invite Jesus to use your home and resources in the way he wants for the sake of his Kingdom. Let us move to the next step and look at the practical issues we face when we open our doors.

Be Prepared

When you open your home to be a place where the risen Lord is invited to visit and minister to your family and friends on a regular basis, you will find that he will honor your faith. He promised to be in the midst of his people wherever they meet in his name and he is true to his word. However, there are some very simple practical steps that will make the meetings much better and more effective and productive.

In the North American culture, many travel by car. Make sure that you have planned for parking and that those who come know where they can park. If there is not adequate parking available, it is imperative that creative planning be done and guests car pool to help ease the burden. This is not just a matter of being practical, but it can also have legal consequences. We will look at some legal issues later, but please note the importance of planning for parking. In addition, it should be planned in such a way that the neighbors are respected and that guests not cause problems for them e.g. by blocking driveways.

Before people arrive, it is good to make sure the house is clean and presentable. This does not mean that you have to be perfect, but when you invite people over, make sure that the house is clean and that those who come will have a place to sit during the meeting. Greet guests at the door and welcome them. People need to know where coats are hung and where to put their shoes. People need to feel they are welcome to come. It is also important that people know where the washroom is and that these facilities are clean with enough toilet paper. It is also good to have ample supplies of Kleenex for times of ministry and that people know where to find these.

Some house churches enjoy regular meals together and others occasionally meet around the table. We will talk more about the inclusion of meals later, but let us first focus on the practical aspects. If a meal will be served, make sure that everyone knows what is expected in advance, particularly if it is a shared meal with guests expected to bring food. If you as host will prepare the meal, make sure that you are ready and that the guests can relax. Depending on the time and costs, it is sometimes better to simply share light refreshments instead of a full meal. We often have coffee and tea with or without something to eat as guests arrive. Whatever you do, plan ahead unless you have a special gift of hospitality that allows for spontaneous decisions that will not disrupt the flow of the meeting.

It is also good to have guests know if there are specific expectations and rules. This is particularly important when new people come who may not be aware of such things. It is also vital to have parents know what is expected of children, e.g. whether they stay in the meeting and if they are free to go to other rooms and what is off limits. Again, we will talk about the children and how they can and should be included later, but here we simply focus on the practical planning. If children are part of the meetings, you have to prepare for them and make sure they know they are accepted and welcomed.

In addition to these very practical preparations, it is just as vital to be spiritually prepared for the meetings. First, and foremost, it is imperative that you prepare the home spiritually, just as you do physically. This is done in advance by spending time in worship and prayer, as you wait for the guests to arrive. One of the home churches that walked in relationship with us when we started out, was Christ's Lighthouse in Georgetown, Ontario. They met at the house of Roger and Ginette. They had a specific night of intercession during the week and prior to their meeting on Sunday morning the intercessors came together and spent time in prayer. Often this time of prayer simply "spilled over" in the meeting as the others arrived. Roger had a specific room in his house that the Lord led him to set aside as a prayer closet, where he and Ginette met with the Lord regularly. While the intercessors were in prayer on Sunday morning in the basement where they met, Roger was spending time with the Lord in his prayer closet, preparing for the meeting.

In our home we pray regularly. I personally love to walk around in prayer seeking the Lord prior to our meeting on Thursday evening. Eda will often worship with music and flags in preparation. It is wonderful to pray for each person coming prior to the meeting and intercede for him or her before the throne of God. In this way the soil is prepared for whatever the Spirit wants to do in each life and the seed can fall in fertile ground. When we travel to home churches to meet, we do the same. We spend time in prayer seeking God's wisdom and grace and praying for his guidance. It is often during the time of preparation in prayer that the Spirit will prepare you to minister effectively to the needs of those for whom you prayed in advance. As you pray for them, you become sensitive to pick up their needs and the Spirit can use you in effective ways or guide you to ask a specific person to minister to the need.

The most important thing is to open the door for Jesus to be present. In our North American culture, we tend to be very individualistic in our approach and interpretation of Scripture. Most of us know the words of Jesus to the church in Laodicea as recorded in Revelation 3:20:

> *Here I am! I stand at the door and knock. If anyone hears my voice and opens the door, I will come in and eat with him, and he with me.*

In our culture we simply make this into a personal issue between an individual and Jesus. However, the context is very clear that Jesus was talking to the church in Laodicea and he was standing outside the door of this church! We cannot have a meeting of the Church without the risen Lord in our midst. Therefore, it is absolutely vital that in the preparation for the meeting, I open the door for Jesus and invite him in. He is to be the guest of honor and the one to whom I submit the leadership of the meeting. With that we need to look at the matter of leadership of the meeting, but one quick observation: When you invite Jesus in, he will show up for sure! However, he has been known to come in unexpected ways and you will often recognize him as you reach out to someone in need in the meeting. He spoke about that in Matthew 25:34-40:

> *Then the King will say to those on his right, 'Come, you who are blessed by my Father; take your inheritance, the kingdom prepared for you since the creation of the world. For I was hungry and you gave me something to eat, I was thirsty and you gave me something to drink, I was a stranger and you invited me in, I needed clothes and you clothed me, I was sick and you looked after me, I was in prison and you came to visit me.'*

> *Then the righteous will answer him, 'Lord, when did we see you hungry and feed you, or thirsty and give you something to drink? When did we see you a stranger and invite you in, or needing clothes and clothe you?*

*When did we see you sick or in prison and
go to visit you?'*

*The King will reply, 'I tell you the truth,
whatever you did for one of the least of these
brothers of mine, you did for me.'*

Not only that, Jesus has been known to challenge the host when he was invited to meetings, e.g. when he was a guest at the house of Simon as recorded in Luke 7:36-50. Thus, be prepared to be challenged and even stretched by Jesus as you invite him to meet your friends in your home. But for now, let us move past the preparations to the issue of leading the church.

Leadership in the House Church

Let us start with the very real and practical issues. First it is important to know that the hosts do not have to be the leaders. Thus, you can open your doors and have the church meet in your house without having to be the leader. Someone else may be called to lead the church but may not have the best suited home to host a regular meeting. At the same time, you could lead the church meeting at your home. The main thing to remember is that the Church is a body and the members have different gifts. The gift of hospitality is vital and no home can serve as meeting place for the church without this gift. Someone in the body must have this gift and be released to flow in the gift. Likewise, there must be good and reliable leadership.

In our experience the best (but by no means only) leadership is when a married couple works together. As indicated in brackets, this is not absolutely necessary, but we find it works best for obvious reasons. In the brokenness of family life, which is rampant in our Western culture, there is power and authority that is released when a couple works in unity and sets an example of cooperation in ministry and leadership. I am also convinced that with the lack of spiritual fathers in particular, house churches where male leadership is properly expressed and practiced will radically transform many homes and families. This leadership is best shown in the way a man works in unity with his wife within the ministry, thus demonstrating the relationship between Christ and the church to the body and to the world as we read in Ephesians 5:21-33:

> *Submit to one another out of reverence for Christ.*
>
> *Wives, submit to your husbands as to the Lord. For the husband is the head of the wife as Christ is the head of the church, his body, of which he is the Savior. Now as the church submits to Christ, so also wives should submit to their husbands in everything.*
>
> *Husbands, love your wives, just as Christ loved the church and gave himself up for her to make her holy, cleansing her by the washing with water through the word, and to present her to himself as a radiant church, without stain or wrinkle or any other blemish, but holy and blameless. In this same way, husbands ought to love their wives as their own bodies. He who loves his wife loves himself. After all, no one ever hated his own body, but he feeds and cares*

for it, just as Christ does the church - for we are members of his body. "For this reason, a man will leave his father and mother and be united to his wife, and the two will become one flesh." This is a profound mystery - but I am talking about Christ and the church. However, each one of you also must love his wife as he loves himself, and the wife must respect her husband.

As we said, the leadership does not have to be a couple, but we have seen that it works best that way. It has the added advantage that ministry needs can be met without the problems that arise when e.g. the leadership is male and there are ministry needs that should be handled by a female. It is best if couples minister together.

Regardless of who is in leadership, it is of the utmost importance that leadership comes through servant hood. This is a Kingdom principle, which I have fully discussed in other books, and it cannot be ignored. True leaders are first and foremost servants. They have to walk in humility. Authority comes through relationship demonstrated in being a servant. Jesus outlined this very clearly in Matthew 20:25-28:

Jesus called them together and said, "You know that the rulers of the Gentiles lord it over them, and their high officials exercise authority over them. Not so with you. Instead, whoever wants to become great among you must be your servant,

and whoever wants to be first must be your
slave - just as the Son of Man did not come
to be served, but to serve, and to give his life
as a ransom for many."

When you lead a home church there are some very practical issues to keep in mind. First and foremost, it is to provide opportunities for Jesus to meet with his family. The meetings should be Christ centered. This is why it is vital as leader to spend time with the Lord and seek him for the direction of each meeting. I am convinced that seeking the Lord in advance allows the Spirit to flow with much more ease than simply hoping that we will experience the power, and presence of the Spirit by getting together. At the same time there needs to be openness and a sensitivity to make changes if needed. There is a fine balance between structure and freedom and as leader one has to be sensitive to the Spirit. Without planning the gatherings very quickly become chaotic and when we miss the Spirit, the life is gone and dead meetings do not attract and keep people.

Leaders do not flow in the same gifts and the meetings will usually reflect the main gifts of the leaders. Those with pastoral gifts tend to attract people who need a shepherd and who might be hurting. The person with a gift for evangelism will seek unbelievers and lead them to the Lord with the result that there will be many baby Christians in the home. Those with a teaching gift will gather those who seek to grow in knowledge. Prophetic leaders tend to lead people who are visionary. **This is to**

be expected and is not wrong in itself. However, in leadership one has to be very careful not to ignore the other gifts of the Spirit. It is very important not to make the meetings into a place where the leader's need to flow in his or her primary gift becomes the purpose of the meeting. This is why it helps to have a couple as leaders, for it often brings more balance. More than that, true servant leaders will recognize the fact that their personal needs are not to be the center, but that they are there first and foremost to serve the other members.

It is important to recognize that the key gifts of the leader can easily be misused with good intentions. Every gift can be exercised in a positive or in a negative way. To be honest, most times there is a mix of the positive and negative. Let us illustrate with specific examples, for this is vital to understand and to put into practice. In a church-planting situation we worked with a wonderful man who was one of the most gifted pastors I ever met. Those who were hurting were attracted to him and he ministered with incredible patience and love. However, this gift also became the very outlet for his own personal need to be a pastor. As a result, he would not release those who got healed and he was over protective. The time spent on keeping all in the fold and the personal time given to each one meant that the group could not grow in numbers. In addition, most who came were kept from growing beyond spiritual infancy, very much like children with an over protective parent. The group did not grow and the gifts of the members were not encouraged. Another example is the leader who is first and foremost a teacher. This is often visibly displayed in the fact that the meeting is set up like a lecture hall or classroom and the leader dominates the discussion. It is little different from the "endless Sunday School lessons" taught in many churches with no visible and practical spiritual growth, nor bringing forth fruit that makes a difference to someone's life. **Please note that we need both pastoral care and teaching, but if the gift becomes the way to serve the needs and aspirations of the leader, it is out of order.**

Thus, it is vital for the leaders to seek the Lord on the direction of each meeting and to ensure that the members are served as Jesus taught his disciples. The authority of a leader comes by way of service. It is very enlightening to read how Paul spoke about his authority as he wrote to the Corinthians who literally made his life difficult: First and most importantly he appealed to them as a spiritual father as we read in 1 Corinthians 4:14-15:

> *I am not writing this to shame you, but to warn you, as my dear children. Even though you have ten thousand guardians in Christ, you do not have many fathers, for in Christ Jesus I became your father through the gospel.*

Then in 2 Corinthians 10:8 and again in 2 Corinthians 13:5-10 he wrote:

For even if I boast somewhat freely about the authority the Lord gave us for building you up rather than pulling you down, I will not be ashamed of it.

Examine yourselves to see whether you are in the faith; test yourselves. Do you not realize that Christ Jesus is in you - unless, of course, you fail the test? And I trust that you will discover that we have not failed the test. Now we pray to God that you will not do anything wrong. Not that people will see that we have stood the test but that you will do what is right even though we may seem to have failed. For we cannot do anything against the truth, but only for the truth. We are glad whenever we are weak but you are strong; and our prayer is for your perfection. This is why I write these things when I am absent, that when I come, I may not have to be harsh in my use of authority - the authority the Lord gave me for building you up, not for tearing you down.

One of the most important things in leading a home church is to use one's gifts in leadership to build those entrusted to your care as a servant of Christ. The authority of leadership comes through the service of building others up in the name of Christ. Whether we teach, prophesy, minister to needs, admonish or even

rebuke, it has to be to build the members of the body and serve our Lord by caring for every member.

Let us look at this from another angle. When Jesus gave the great commission as recorded in Matthew 28:18-20 he said:

> *"All authority in heaven and on earth has been given to me. Therefore, go and make disciples of all nations, baptizing them in the name of the Father and of the Son and of the Holy Spirit, and teaching them to obey everything I have commanded you. And surely, I am with you always, to the very end of the age."*

A vital part of the Great Commission is to make disciples of all nations. The term "to make disciples" literally means to get the new believers to become students who are then taught to obey everything Jesus taught. The idea is to get the believers to learn to walk in The Way. In this process it is very important to be filled with the Spirit and learn to exercise one's spiritual gifts. As leaders, one of the most important objectives is to help every believer in the church know his or her gifts and to ensure that those gifts are released for Kingdom service. The small intimate setting of the home church is the ideal place where gifts are identified and every person is encouraged to grow up in Christ by using the gifts of the Spirit to strengthen the body. Leadership means that we serve the body by helping each person to grow to his or her full potential. Therefore, as leader my specific gifts must be applied first and foremost to build each person individually and the group corporately. In the process I need to be sensitive to the Spirit. By building relationships with those entrusted to my care with a heart of servant hood, I receive the authority to build the lives of those in the church.

Jesus primarily spent time with twelve disciples over a span of about three years to teach and train them about the Kingdom of heaven. Let us take a few notes on how Jesus led this group, for if we grasp the principles, we will know how to have churches meet in our homes. First, he spent time in prayer as he sought the disciples. The Spirit knows who will best lead whom. In fact, no church should be started without the guidance of the Spirit. In calling some of the disciples, Jesus prophetically spoke into their lives at specific times, e.g. when he called the fishermen, he implicitly told them that as they follow him, they would learn to be fishers of men. Later when Peter made the confession of faith that Jesus was the Messiah, Jesus prophetically changed his name from Simon to Peter. He saw in Peter a rock that would be instrumental in becoming an apostle (a sent one) to lay the foundation of the church preaching the truth about Jesus. On another occasion he saw the weakness in Peter that would lead to his denial of his Lord and prophetically foretold this, but also said (Luke 22:31-32):

> *"Simon, Simon, Satan has asked to sift you as wheat. But I have prayed for you, Simon that your faith may not fail. And*

when you have turned back, strengthen your brothers."

Jesus as leader saw the strengths and the weaknesses of Peter and through prophetic words encouraged him, stretched him and built him up. When needed, he spoke very strong words, but for the most part he walked alongside him and the other disciples building them up and encouraging them. He modeled leadership by being a servant and by investing his life in theirs. When Peter was to face a major crisis in his faith, Jesus prophetically prepared him for that and spoke forth his restoration. After the resurrection he sought Peter again and turned his life around at the very place where he was first called, as we read in John 21, when Peter had made the decision to return to his old familiar way of life as fisherman. In pastoral love Jesus not only restored Peter, but also taught him how to be a true pastor caring for the sheep – especially the little lambs. The fruit of this is seen in Peter's letters, e.g., 1 Peter 5:1-4:

To the elders among you, I appeal as a fellow elder, a witness of Christ's sufferings and one who will also share in the glory to be revealed: Be shepherds of God's flock that is under your care, serving as overseers – not because you must, but because you are willing as God wants you to be; not greedy for money, but eager to serve; not lording it over those entrusted to you, but being examples to the flock. And when the Chief

Shepherd appears, you will receive the crown of glory that will never fade away.

Talking about Jesus, it is important to see how he taught. He rarely spoke long. He taught in simple ways telling stories. Most of the time the stories were taken directly from the immediate context and the lessons applied to life. The disciples learned to live life by walking in The Way. Those that walked with Jesus were recognized by their lifestyle as having been with Jesus as we read in Acts 4:13-20:

> <u>*When they saw the courage of Peter and John and realized that they were unschooled, ordinary men, they were astonished and they took note that these men had been with Jesus.*</u> *But since they could see the man who had been healed standing there with them, there was nothing they could say. So, they ordered them to withdraw from the Sanhedrin and then conferred together. "What are we going to do with these men?" they asked. "Everybody living in Jerusalem knows they have done an outstanding miracle, and we cannot deny it. But to stop this thing from spreading any further among the people, we must warn these men to speak no longer to anyone in this name."*
>
> *Then they called them in again and commanded them not to speak or teach at all in the name of Jesus. But Peter and John*

> *replied, "Judge for yourselves whether it is right in God's sight to obey you rather than God. For we cannot help speaking about what we have seen and heard."*

Those who were with Jesus learned to walk in The Way and thus became known as the people of The Way. They had learnt to walk as Jesus walked and speak as Jesus spoke and do as Jesus did. He taught by example. He taught the disciples to look at the world and people through the eyes of God's love. When he was at the house of Simon the Pharisee, he used the interruption when the broken prostitute poured the expensive perfume on him and sobbed at his feet, to teach them about the love of God and how important it is to care for the hurting. When he sat at the temple, he saw the widow dropping two pennies in the offering and taught the principles of Kingdom giving compared to giving from the overflow. When he was pushed and shoved in the crowd on the way to Jairus' home, he sensed her presence and stopped to minister to the woman with the issue of blood. In this he taught the disciples how to be sensitive when healing virtue is flowing from you. In the process he set the example of what it is to walk in the anointing with a pastor's heart, for he did this because he had compassion on the people.

He did not just teach them these lessons, but he encouraged them to go and do the same. He sent them out to put into practice what they and seen and heard. Afterwards he sat down with them and then had opportunities to talk about these things and how they were successful. He was willing as leader to allow them to go on their own and do the work of ministry. He trained and released them. He encouraged them to do the work of ministry, even when they tried and failed. It is interesting to note that the occasion where the disciples tried to do what they had learnt and failed. Let us read that and note Jesus' response as recorded in Mark 9:14-29:

> When they came to the other disciples, they saw a large crowd around them and the teachers of the law arguing with them. As soon as all the people saw Jesus, they were overwhelmed with wonder and ran to greet him.
>
> "What are you arguing with them about?" he asked.
>
> A man in the crowd answered, "Teacher, I brought you my son, who is possessed by a spirit that has robbed him of speech. Whenever it seizes him, it throws him to the ground. He foams at the mouth, gnashes his teeth and becomes rigid. I asked your disciples to drive out the spirit, but they could not."
>
> "O unbelieving generation," Jesus replied, "how long shall I stay with you? How long shall I put up with you? Bring the boy to me."

So, they brought him. When the spirit saw Jesus, it immediately threw the boy into a convulsion. He fell to the ground and rolled around, foaming at the mouth.

Jesus asked the boy's father, "How long has he been like this?"

"From childhood," he answered. "It has often thrown him into fire or water to kill him. But if you can do anything, take pity on us and help us."

"'If you can'?" said Jesus. "Everything is possible for him who believes."

Immediately the boy's father exclaimed, "I do believe; help me overcome my unbelief!"

When Jesus saw that a crowd was running to the scene, he rebuked the evil spirit. "You deaf and mute spirit," he said, "I command you, come out of him and never enter him again."

The spirit shrieked, convulsed him violently and came out. The boy looked so much like a corpse that many said, "He's dead." But Jesus took him by the hand and lifted him to his feet, and he stood up.

After Jesus had gone indoors, his disciples asked him privately, "Why couldn't we drive it out?"

He replied, "This kind can come out only by prayer."

Why is this story so important? Listen – Jesus allowed his disciples to engage in ministry before they were fully trained! He sent them out and taught them by example and by sending them into the world. When they encountered something they could not handle, he explained the next step to them. They had on the job training with encouragement – to use Paul's terminology they were being built up for ministry in the world! That is what discipleship is all about and that is one of the primary objects of meeting together.

The key issue about leading the home church is to see each person and the group through the eyes of Jesus. Once you do that, you ask the Spirit to seek what God wants to accomplish in the individual and corporate lives of those who are part of the gathering and what are his priorities. With that established, you work towards that objective as led by the Spirit – if you need to teach, teach as he directs; if you need to speak prophetically, do so; if you need to minister, do so. In the process, be open and encourage others in their gifts to meet needs. Always work to build up the body in every way. <u>Church happens in your home when you allow Jesus to work through you and through every one</u>

present, to build one another up and to allow the glory of God to shine in and through the lives of his people.

This is so simple many cannot believe it. To lead the church is as simple as being a servant to God's people as he directs to build them up. It is as simple as asking the Spirit to open the eyes of every person to see as Jesus does and to respond as he would. It is as simple as trusting the Spirit to work in and through you to accomplish his work to the glory of the Father. It is as simple as being a child in the presence of a loving father and enjoying the moment with friends.

For some as you read this, every religious spirit is moving and shouting in your ears. These spirits will tell you it cannot be "church." However, seek the Spirit and listen with a childlike faith to this: Can you experience church any more than being in the very presence with Jesus, being filled and led by the Spirit and seeking to serve him as he directs for that moment in order that the Father be glorified?

This is why we started by saying that the first issue you have to settle is that the church meeting in your house is the church – period! The issue above is tied to that. The biggest problem for the home church is that many try to transplant the church program from the church building to the home. Doing that is simply playing religious games. The moment you try to do that you are back into religion and it is deadly. Then the leader becomes "the pastor" and you are back to square one with the Levitical order.

Leadership is simply to allow Jesus to visit his people in your home and follow his direction. It is never boring! Just think what happened in the early church when they met together! In fact, let us go there and take a good look at their meetings!

Meeting With Jesus and Your Friends

In the Book of Acts, we read about some of the early Christian meetings. The first took place immediately following Pentecost as recorded in Acts 2:42-47:

> *They devoted themselves to the apostles'*
> *teaching and to the fellowship, to the*
> *breaking of bread and to prayer. Everyone*
> *was filled with awe, and many wonders*
> *and miraculous signs were done by the*
> *apostles. All the believers were together and*
> *had everything in common. Selling their*
> *possessions and goods, they gave to anyone*
> *as he had need. Every day they continued*
> *to meet together in the temple courts. They*
> *broke bread in their homes and ate together*
> *with glad and sincere hearts, praising God*
> *and enjoying the favor of all the people. And*
> *the Lord added to their number daily those*
> *who were being saved.*

Thus, from the beginning they met in homes, although they also used the availability of the temple courts for a while. The latter did not last, as persecution drove many out and within a few decades the temple was destroyed with the destruction of Jerusalem in 70 AD. More importantly at this point is to see what they did as they gathered. In the passage above we find that they devoted themselves to the apostles teaching and to the fellowship, to the breaking of bread and to prayer. Then we read again that they broke bread in their homes and ate together with glad and sincere hearts, praising God and enjoying the favor of all the people.

Let us begin with these things. When they met these early believers sat around a table and shared a meal. Bread was a staple, but also used with wine at most meals. Breaking bread together in the homes meant they ate together and, in the process, they remembered the death and resurrection of our Lord in communion. The fellowship centered on the person and work of Jesus. They met in his name and he was present, for he promised that where two or three are gathered in his name he would be present. They prayed together and praised God. Where a need became known they met the need by giving, even if it meant selling possessions and goods to be able to give to anyone as he had need. In a word, they cared for one another in tangible ways.

Something else needs to be noted: They devoted themselves to the apostles' teaching. What was the apostles' teaching and how did they learn this? The apostles laid the foundations for the church and we are talking about foundational teachings. We read in Hebrews 6:1-2:

> *Therefore, let us leave <u>the elementary teachings about Christ</u> and go on to maturity, not laying again <u>the foundation of repentance from acts that lead to death, and of faith in God, instruction about baptisms, the laying on of hands, the resurrection of the dead, and eternal judgment.</u>*

These are very basic issues. We also find that Paul wrote to the Corinthians about his approach when he planted the church and said in 1 Corinthians 2:1-5:

> *When I came to you, brothers, I did not come with eloquence or superior wisdom as I proclaimed to you the testimony about God. <u>For I resolved to know nothing while I was with you except Jesus Christ and him crucified.</u> I came to you in weakness and fear, and with much trembling. My message and my preaching were not with wise and persuasive words, but with a demonstration of the Spirit's power, so that your faith might not rest on men's wisdom, but on God's power.*

This is very much in line with the recorded teaching and preaching of the apostles as we find examples in the book of Acts, e.g. Acts 5:27-33:

Having brought the apostles, they made them appear before the Sanhedrin to be questioned by the high priest. "We gave you strict orders not to teach in this name," he said. "<u>Yet you have filled Jerusalem with your teaching</u> and are determined to make us guilty of this man's blood."

<u>*Peter and the other apostles replied: "We must obey God rather than men! The God of our fathers raised Jesus from the dead - whom you had killed by hanging him on a tree. God exalted him to his own right hand as Prince and Savior that he might give repentance and forgiveness of sins to Israel. We are witnesses of these things, and so is the Holy Spirit, whom God has given to those who obey him."*</u>

We can quote passage after passage to show that the apostles' teaching was focused on Jesus and the story of his life, death and resurrection. Tied to this teaching was the presence of the Holy Spirit, for the message included the witness of the Spirit and about the Spirit. In fact, it is vital that we take a closer look at this as we try to understand what the apostles' teaching was all about. As we saw above Paul wrote to the Corinthians that he determined to teach and preach nothing except Jesus Christ and him crucified. Directly following that he wrote in 1 Corinthians 2:6-16:

We do, however, speak a message of wisdom among the mature, but not the wisdom of this age or of the rulers of this age, who are coming to nothing. No, we speak of God's secret wisdom, a wisdom that has been hidden and that God destined for our glory before time began. None of the rulers of this age understood it, for if they had, they would not have crucified the Lord of glory. However, as it is written:

"No eye has seen,
no ear has heard,
no mind has conceived
what God has prepared for those who love him" -

but God has revealed it to us by his Spirit.

The Spirit searches all things, even the deep things of God. For who among men knows the thoughts of a man except the man's spirit within him? In the same way no one knows the thoughts of God except the Spirit of God. We have not received the spirit of the world but the Spirit who is from God, that we may understand what God has freely given us.

This is what we speak, not in words taught us by human wisdom but in words taught by the Spirit, expressing spiritual truths in spiritual words. The man without the Spirit does not accept the things that come from the Spirit of God, for they are foolishness to him, and he cannot understand them, because they are spiritually discerned. The spiritual man makes judgments about all things, but he himself is not subject to any man's judgment:

"For who has known the mind of the Lord that he may instruct him?"

But we have the mind of Christ.

The teaching of the apostles included the presence and power of the Spirit to reveal the truth to those being taught. Without openness to the Spirit, the truth could not be revealed. They taught revelation truth. They spoke about the Kingdom of God as Jesus did and told the story of the Messianic King who died on the cross and was raised on the third day. This message opened the door to enter into the Kingdom through repentance and forgiveness of sins. Those who accepted the message were radically changed for they became born again, just as Jesus said to Nicodemus, John 3:5-8:

"I tell you the truth, no one can enter the kingdom of God unless he is born of water and the Spirit. Flesh gives birth to flesh, but the Spirit gives birth to spirit. You should not be surprised at my saying, 'You must be born again.' The wind blows wherever it

<u>*pleases. You hear its sound, but you cannot*</u>
<u>*tell where it comes from or where it is going.*</u>
<u>*So it is with everyone born of the Spirit.*"</u>

In obedience they were baptized in water and in the Spirit. They became filled with the Spirit and equipped by the Spirit, clothed with power from on high that enabled them to be effective witnesses to the spiritual truth of this Good News about the Kingdom, just as the risen Lord said in Acts 1:8:

> *But you will receive power when the Holy Spirit comes on you; and you will be my witnesses in Jerusalem, and in all Judea and Samaria, and to the ends of the earth.*

Filled with the Spirit they learned to walk in The Way. When they met, they shared meals and broke bread in remembrance of the Lord who came to this world to die on the cross for them. They talked about their everyday lives and encouraged one another in word and in deed. In this the teaching of the apostles was very important, for it was about the Lord and what he said and did. The apostles' teaching helped them to find answers to enable them to live their lives worthy of the gospel as Paul encouraged the believers in Philippians 1:27-28:

> *Whatever happens, conduct yourselves in a manner worthy of the gospel of Christ. Then, whether I come and see you or only hear about you in my absence, I will know that you stand firm in one spirit,*

*contending as one man for the faith of the
gospel without being frightened in any way
by those who oppose you.*

When they met, they talked around the table eating together. They offered advice where needed, gave encouragement for those who faced difficulties, prayed for the church and laid hands on the sick. When someone needed better grounding in the faith it was done by other members as we read in Acts 18:24-26:

> *Meanwhile a Jew named Apollos, a native
> of Alexandria, came to Ephesus. He was a
> learned man, with a thorough knowledge
> of the Scriptures. <u>He had been instructed in
> the way of the Lord, and he spoke with great
> fervor and taught about Jesus accurately,
> though he knew only the baptism of John.
> He began to speak boldly in the synagogue.
> When Priscilla and Aquila heard him, they
> invited him to their home and explained to
> him the way of God more adequately.</u>*

In the same way we read how Paul met disciples who needed better grounding in the faith regarding the Holy Spirit in Acts 19:1-7:

> *While Apollos was at Corinth, Paul took
> the road through the interior and arrived
> at Ephesus. There he found some disciples
> and asked them, "Did you receive the Holy
> Spirit when you believed?"*

They answered, "No, we have not even heard that there is a Holy Spirit."

So Paul asked, "Then what baptism did you receive?"

"John's baptism," they replied.

Paul said, "John's baptism was a baptism of repentance. He told the people to believe in the one coming after him, that is, in Jesus." On hearing this, they were baptized into the name of the Lord Jesus. When Paul placed his hands on them, the Holy Spirit came on them, and they spoke in tongues and prophesied. There were about twelve men in all.

Earlier we noticed that the elementary teachings included the teaching on baptisms and the laying on of hands. In the story above we find a practical illustration of these teachings and how it changed the lives of the disciples.

Most importantly: Notice how the teaching was done in those days. There were formal settings, e.g. just following the story recalled above, we read how Paul rented a lecture hall and held daily discussions there. However, for the most part the teaching took place the same way Jesus taught his disciples: It was informal and arose out of practical everyday real-life situations. It was often in the midst of discussions and in response to questions. Also important to notice, is

that with Jesus the questions were very often related to observations of his lifestyle that did not conform to the religious traditions as taught by religious leaders or to the power and authority in which he operated. The same was true for the disciples as they were often questioned about their authority and became known for their Way of Life.

Having said that and reading the letters to the churches, it is very clear that teaching was seldom done in the style and way we practice in the Western world, least of all a weekly sermon where all sat down to listen to a pastor. It came out of real-life situations and as they met in the homes, sharing their lives with others, the teaching took place. The gathering of the church was intimately linked to talking and encouraging one another as the stories were shared while eating. Teaching was for the most part the practical advice from others in the light of the Kingdom realities and truths they learned from one another and from itinerant apostles, prophets, teachers, pastors and evangelists. The idea was to gather in the name of Jesus and experience his presence while encouraging one another to grow in effectiveness as they walk in The Way. It is very enlightening to see how the word "teach" is used in the New Testament when referring to the church. Apart from the basic foundations that were laid by the apostles as described above, the word is used in reference to living in the world as believers. This is very clearly seen in the letters to Timothy and Titus where Paul wrote to them what they should be teaching, e.g. Titus 2:1-3:1:

You must teach what is in accord with sound doctrine. Teach the older men to be temperate, worthy of respect, self-controlled, and sound in faith, in love and in endurance.

Likewise, teach the older women to be reverent in the way they live, not to be slanderers or addicted to much wine, but to teach what is good. *Then they can train the younger women* to love their husbands and children, to be self-controlled and pure, to be busy at home, to be kind, and to be subject to their husbands, so that no one will malign the word of God.

Similarly, encourage the young men to be self -controlled. In everything set them an example by doing what is good. In your teaching show integrity, seriousness and soundness of speech that cannot be condemned, so that those who oppose you may be ashamed because they have nothing bad to say about us.

Teach slaves to be subject to their masters in everything, to try to please them, not to talk back to them, and not to steal from them, but to show that they can be fully trusted, so that in every way they will make the teaching about God our Savior attractive.

For the grace of God that brings salvation has appeared to all men. It teaches us to say "No" to ungodliness and worldly passions, and to live self-controlled, upright and godly lives in this present age, while we wait for the blessed hope - the glorious appearing of our great God and Savior, Jesus Christ, who gave himself for us to redeem us from all wickedness and to purify for himself a people that are his very own, eager to do what is good.

These, then, are the things you should teach. Encourage and rebuke with all authority. Do not let anyone despise you.

It is not too difficult to get the picture. Once foundational issues are in place, they did not need to be repeated endlessly. In fact, that was why the author to the Hebrews wrote to and challenged the readers in Hebrews 5:11-6:3:

We have much to say about this, but it is hard to explain because you are slow to learn. In fact, though by this time you ought to be teachers, you need someone to teach you the elementary truths of God's word all over again. You need milk, not solid food! Anyone who lives on milk, being still an infant, is not acquainted with the teaching about righteousness. But solid food is for the mature, who by constant use have trained themselves to distinguish good from evil.

> *Therefore, let us leave the elementary teachings about Christ and go on to maturity,* not laying again the foundation of repentance from acts that lead to death, and of faith in God, instruction about baptisms, the laying on of hands, the resurrection of the dead, and eternal judgment. And God permitting, we will do so.

The idea of teaching was to encourage each one to live up to the call of Christ in his or her life. Each person was to learn to walk in The Way. This is best done in a small setting where the teacher can talk to the disciple and where there can be a focus on the key individual issues being faced. Like Jesus did with his disciples, much of the teaching happened as they talked at mealtime or wherever. Wisdom gained through practical application was shared as they discussed things while at table – and major revelation flowed at such times as we know e.g. from the last meal Jesus had with his disciples as recorded by John.

Let us get the picture in perspective for a moment: These early believers met regularly with one another in their homes. When it was possible, they shared a meal and broke bread in remembrance of Jesus. As they met, they shared their lives with one another. They talked and encouraged one another, meeting needs in practical ways and reminding one another of the apostles' teachings. They were taught and encouraged to walk in The Way as they shared and imparted knowledge and wisdom to one another. The purpose was to allow each one to grow in every way according to his or her call and gifts. This is why when they met together each one contributed something as we find in 1 Corinthians 14:26:

What then shall we say, brothers? <u>When you come together, everyone has a hymn, or a word of instruction, a revelation, a tongue or an interpretation. All of these must be done for the strengthening of the church.</u>

Various gifts were given to each member for the purpose of supporting and encouraging the whole body, or as we read above "for the strengthening of the church." This is why the members had to be knowledgeable about the gifts as we read in 1 Corinthians 12:1-7:

<u>Now about spiritual gifts, brothers, I do not want you to be ignorant.</u> You know that when you were pagans, somehow or other you were influenced and led astray to mute idols. Therefore, I tell you that no one who is speaking by the Spirit of God says, "Jesus be cursed," and no one can say, "Jesus is Lord," except by the Holy Spirit.

There are different kinds of gifts, but the same Spirit. There are different kinds of service, but the same Lord. There are different kinds of working, but the same God works all of them in all men.

> *Now to each one the manifestation of the*
> *Spirit is given for the common good.*

We find the same message in Paul's letter to the Romans in chapter 12:3-8:

> *For by the grace given me I say to every one of you: Do not think of yourself more highly than you ought, but rather think of yourself with sober judgment, in accordance with the measure of faith God has given you. Just as each of us has one body with many members, and these members do not all have the same function, so in Christ we who are many form one body, and each member belongs to all the others. We have different gifts, according to the grace given us. If a man's gift is prophesying, let him use it in proportion to his faith. If it is serving, let him serve; if it is teaching, let him teach; if it is encouraging, let him encourage; if it is contributing to the needs of others, let him give generously; if it is leadership, let him govern diligently; if it is showing mercy, let him do it cheerfully.*

The teaching contained in these verses is very important in order to grasp what took place at the meetings when the members came together. We already saw how they all came to give something to encourage one another – a hymn, a prophetic word, a tongue or interpretation, instruction, etc. In the light of Romans 12 we understand that each gift was to be released **in accordance with the level of faith of the person.** This is why Paul wrote that no one should think too highly of himself, but soberly and in accordance with his own measure of faith. Each one belongs to the others in this body and each has a responsibility to everyone else. Thus, if the admonition is applied, it would mean that the least will be released to minister to the others and it has to be received and encouraged. In practical terms it means that baby Christians were encouraged by the others to practice their gifts and in this way each one was encouraged and could grow in faith. In fact, the least had to be treated as the greatest in the Kingdom.

Let us cut to the chase here: When the believers met together, they often shared a meal and broke bread in remembrance of Jesus. This kept them focused on Jesus as the center of the meeting. They came to share according to their gifts and level of faith and the fellowship was focused on building each one up and encouraging one another in the faith. Thus, they cared for one another and encouraged each other by exercising their gifts. A primary focus was to help each one to live in the world as a witness by walking in The Way. The meeting of the church was to build each member to grow up in all things into Christ who is the head of his body, the church.

With that let us move on to how we can put the same into practice. Frankly, it is not difficult to do at all. In the words of the heading for this chapter, it is simply to allow your friends to meet with Jesus in your presence in your home. So, having prepared earlier by spending time with Jesus you know what to expect.

Let me illustrate this with specific examples. First stay true to who you are and how God created you. We do need to plan and seek God, but some are by nature more spontaneous than others, who need to be very prepared to allow them the freedom to relax and move as the Spirit leads. Do not try to do something that is totally out of character, especially as you begin. Personally, I prefer to begin with a time around a table or with some refreshments – whether a meal or simply something to drink. It allows for people to open up and share their lives and very often as they talk and share the Spirit will reveal some needs or allow specific questions to arise. As we talk and listen, by being open to the Spirit, we get direction and opportunity to respond to the specific issues. In the response we always seek the Spirit not just to find answers, but also to allow the different gifts to be exercised. The key is to allow the members of the body to do body ministry.

As we have done this, we have found that the Spirit is indeed like the wind and often moves in a way we never expected. We have had times when we were led simply to stay around the table and pray for one another and the needs that arose and were brought up. There have been times when a specific issue led us to devote most of the time to teaching and we simply closed with prayer. We have had times when we were led to begin with worship and the Spirit ministered while we praised the Lord. Other times we had powerful prophetic words being released from within the body to one another and ended in spontaneous worship and praise. There are times when we sense the need to teach and will spend most of the time doing that.

Some people find it easy to lead and are experienced, so that it is easy to guide the gathering. When you begin and have never done it, plan ahead and simply be open to the Spirit to change when it is needed. **To me the simple way to lead the house church is to remember that the real objective is to have Jesus meet your friends in your home.** With that you can never go wrong. Thus, you ask Jesus what he wants to do and plan accordingly. Look at people through his eyes and challenge the others to do the same. As you join together in unity in the Spirit to hear Jesus and worship him, the Spirit will lead you as he promised. As you pray for one another, the Spirit will release the words whether prophetic, evangelistic, exhortation or pastoral. Make sure that every single one is included, from old to young. There is no junior Holy Spirit and even little ones must be included and know they are important and can have the Holy Spirit – and if you have a problem to grasp that, read the Bible! Listen to this amazing statement in Luke 1:39-45:

> *At that time Mary got ready and hurried to a town in the hill country of Judea, where she entered Zechariah's home and greeted Elizabeth. <u>When Elizabeth heard</u>*

> *Mary's greeting, the baby leaped in her womb, and Elizabeth was filled with the Holy Spirit. In a loud voice she exclaimed: "Blessed are you among women, and blessed is the child you will bear! But why am I so favored, that the mother of my Lord should come to me? As soon as the sound of your greeting reached my ears, the baby in my womb leaped for joy.* Blessed is she who has believed that what the Lord has said to her will be accomplished!"

It is amazing how God's Spirit works in intergenerational settings! The Western church misses the greatest opportunity to set the stage for forming the next generation, because of the misplaced belief that the generation gap has to be accepted. That belief has led the programmed church to run separate programs for different groups and ages. The Biblical teaching is that God is a tri-generational God or as we read in the Old Testament, he is the God of Abraham, Isaac and Jacob. By separating the body in different age groups through the Sunday school approach, which also expanded into separate worship events in many churches, we have chosen to separate the members of the body and brought division into the body of Christ. **However, God has not changed and he is still the God of Abraham, Isaac and Jacob. The Holy Spirit works in power when there is unity in the body when we come together and we see that when young and old get together in unity. In fact, as the Third Day Church**

arises there is a specific prophetic word that we need to hear very clearly, recorded in Malachi 4:5-6:

> *"See, I will send you the prophet Elijah before that great and dreadful day of the LORD comes. He will turn the hearts of the fathers to their children, and the hearts of the children to their fathers; or else I will come and strike the land with a curse."*

The most natural place for the generations to come together in unity is around the table in a home. One of the main pictures of the church is that of the family of God. We are seeing amazing witness to the power of the Spirit as old and young come together in unity with the expectation that we are in the times when the promise of Joel first made manifest on the day of Pentecost is able to manifest through old and young as we read in Joel 2:28-32:

> *And afterward,*
> *I will pour out my Spirit on all people.*
> *Your sons and daughters will prophesy,*
> *your old men will dream dreams,*
> *your young men will see visions.*
> *Even on my servants, both men and women,*
> *I will pour out my Spirit in those days.*
> *I will show wonders in the heavens and on the earth,*
> *blood and fire and billows of smoke.*
> *The sun will be turned to darkness and the moon to blood*

> *before the coming of the great and dreadful*
> *day of the LORD.*
> *And everyone who calls on the name of the*
> *LORD will be saved;*
> *for on Mount Zion and in Jerusalem there*
> *will be deliverance,*
> *as the LORD has said, among the survivors*
> *whom the LORD calls.*

The Holy Spirit is for every person – regardless of age, education, race or gender. Let me give you specific examples of the power of intergenerational unity and how the Spirit of God can minister. One night we were in a home seated around the table. There is freedom, for where the Spirit is, is freedom. After the meal the adults were still at table talking, while the children were playing in another room. They vary in age from 9 to 15. As we continued to talk the Spirit brought revelation of some specific issues – and everyone at the table reached for their Bibles. Suddenly the children just came in and joined the conversation about these issues. No one had called them, but the Spirit who wanted to reveal truth to us drew them and they joined us. A while later they were out again, but the Spirit used the "adult discussion" to bring revelation to everyone, including the children.

These same children and young people, with other friends, meet with two mothers once a week after school. It is literally another home church for the mothers and children. Lives are changed as these two mothers simply open the home and allow Jesus to meet them and the young ones. There is no structured program. They simply pray and all expect the Holy Spirit to guide them. Sometimes they worship. Sometimes they share the needs and pray. They move prophetically and encourage one another. The youngest told her mother one morning she felt she needed to stay home from school and spent the day with Jesus. A very cautious and at first skeptical mother sought the Lord and allowed the unusual request. This little 9-year-old spent most of the day in prayer and reading her Bible. That afternoon as the others came in, the mothers who simply trust the Spirit to guide them found they had no idea what to do. This little one came in and announced that she had a message from the Lord. She proceeded to share the word and her message opened the door for a teenager to reveal a problem she had and a major life change was the result.

We can share more examples, but the issue is very simple. Children are part and parcel of the church and when we truly meet as families in home settings, they are as much members of the body as the adults. The Sunday school model built on the Western concept of teaching has done precisely what Jesus did not want to happen, for it has literally forced the children from being touched by the Lord, treating them as second-class citizens. This Western Sunday school model flows from an attitude like that of the disciples who considered the children to be a problem in their "adult setting" as we read in Mark 10:13-16:

> *People were bringing little children to Jesus*
> *to have him touch them, but the disciples*

rebuked them. When Jesus saw this, he was indignant. He said to them, "Let the little children come to me, and do not hinder them, for the kingdom of God belongs to such as these. I tell you the truth, anyone who will not receive the kingdom of God like a little child will never enter it." And he took the children in his arms, put his hands on them and blessed them.

The house church setting is ideal for the generations to come together in unity and is far better to train and teach children, than the Sunday School approach and programs that rarely bring fruit and lead to generational division. The house church setting allows for specific times when the Spirit would direct the leadership to have some minister with the children in another room. With a little creativity even little ones can be part of the body and minister. The Bible and history itself have many examples of children moving in ministry and in power. In the house setting the older Abraham generation is vital to come alongside the Isaac generation to support them and to lay hands on the younger Jacob generation to bless and empower them. It is time in particular for the fathers to turn their hearts to the children so that the children will turn their hearts tot the fathers. In the West we have been living under the curse too long. It is time to practice and live being church in family settings and to abandon the leaky foundations of programmed Sunday school that misses the generational blessing.

This matter is so important that we have to look at it from another angle. As we have seen the early church regularly gathered around a table for meals and when they did, they broke bread together. The term "broke bread" is a reference to the celebration of Communion that was done in remembrance of the death and resurrection of Jesus as he commanded them. When Jesus instituted communion, it happened at the celebration of Passover and in a very real sense he became our Passover lamb. The roots of communion are therefore found in the Old Testament celebration of Passover. As we take a look at the celebration of Passover as recorded in Exodus 12, we find that Moses gave details as to how it is to be observed. It was a feast to be celebrated in a family context with the whole family involved. At the end of the instructions we read in Exodus 12:26-27:

> *And when your children ask you, 'What does this ceremony mean to you?' then tell them, 'It is the Passover sacrifice to the LORD, who passed over the houses of the Israelites in Egypt and spared our homes when he struck down the Egyptians.'*

This is extremely important for in Israel the foundations were taught in a family setting often when a meal was shared at table. In a very literal sense one of the children were to ask the question that would open the door for the father to teach the truth to the family. This is the context of the celebration of communion in the church. It has little to do with a symbolic little wafer or piece of bread followed by a little drop of grape juice being passed along the rows to people seated in the pews or chairs once a month or so at church. There are no rules in Scripture that only an "ordained minister or priest" may handle the holy sacrament and that children may not share in this meal. It is to be a celebration of the family that is best done in a real family context where children sit with their family and friends at the table and where the truths about the life, death and resurrection of our Lord are being taught, while we do this in remembrance of him.

In fact, the key issue addressed in 1 Corinthians 11 about the Lord's Supper has to do with the lack of unity in that particular church. That issue meant that they celebrated communion without recognizing the body of the Lord. In Paul's words in 1 Corinthians 11:27-29:

> *Therefore, whoever eats the bread or drinks the cup of the Lord in an unworthy manner will be guilty of sinning against the body and blood of the Lord. A man ought to examine himself before he eats of the bread and drinks of the cup. For anyone who eats and drinks without recognizing the body of the Lord eats and drinks judgment on himself.*

This passage has nothing to do with whether or not children "understand" in rational terms all that Jesus did for us when he died on the cross (as if adults do!), but it has to do with the fact that it is wrong to celebrate communion with divisions in the body. There must be unity and unity that includes all members – even the little ones. This is best done in a family setting within a house around a table, as that was the place it started and the roots go back to the family observance of Passover. If we follow the Jewish model to teach spiritual truths in a family setting around the table, it is powerful and effective.

Tie to this the blessings that are released from the older to the younger generation as the little ones learn the truths of respecting the fathers and mothers. In a three generational home setting this can be visibly illustrated every time the church meets. The Spirit will also direct times when the older generation speak forth blessings and pray over the little ones. When we meet together, we are very aware of the fact that God is a tri-generational God and that there needs to be a flow from one generation to the other. There is an added advantage in that parents will find positive support in raising their children and those from broken homes benefit immensely when the church becomes a place where positive family relationships are visibly demonstrated.

A little planning goes a long way. Little ones can come with a pillow, blanket and pajamas and sleep when it gets to bedtime. We have Lego that has become part of the family and when little ones come, they enjoy playing with someone else's toys. At times they will be in a room where they play – at times we meet with them present. There is a free flow and they know when they need to be with us and when they can break away. It takes the stress off the parents and we simply spell out the rules. Sometimes they use the Lego to build something in line with what they just learned. We ask questions about their needs and we pray with them for these needs and for their friends. They share their testimonies and we see the power of the Spirit as they learn to walk in The Way in their everyday life at school. This is more exciting than the boring Sunday school lessons with the props to keep the kids busy while the parents have "real church." **There is nothing more powerful and exciting for children and teens than to be full of the Spirit and learn to walk in the Spirit by exercising the gifts of the Spirit. The world does not have anything that can remotely compete with that and this is why they enjoy being part of a real Spirit filled meeting. Add to that the joy of seeing their parents and older people flow in the Spirit and being touched by the Spirit and you will never think of keeping them separate.**

Having said all of that, there is nothing wrong if kids meet separately with others at times and for teens to have more teen-oriented meetings from time to time. However, the house church offers a very powerful place for intergenerational meetings and should be open to encourage that, because unity is essential and it crosses all human barriers. Children also help us to see through Kingdom eyes, for Jesus said in Luke 18:17:

> *I tell you the truth, anyone who will not receive the kingdom of God like a little child will never enter it.*

WORSHIP PRAISE AND PRAYER

Intergenerational meetings with a table and food are not difficult to visualize and many can relate to that. However, when it comes to worship and praise in a home setting, we find that there are practical questions that need to be addressed.

We have seen and experienced different ways of worship in a home setting, from good to poor and from amazing to frustrating. It is important to notice that there are limitations to expressive worship in homes, because of limited space. This has to be taken into account when we plan worship. In addition, the talent pool for leading worship will be smaller and this brings other limitations. In dealing with these issues we need to be practical and at times creative. The very problems we see are often the doors that God open to new opportunities. There are some, whose musical talents may not allow them to lead in a larger gathering, but in a small home setting God opens the door for them and they grow and mature. Having said that, it is also very important to note that lack of talent can be deadly in both a small house setting as well as in a larger meeting. The object of leading worship is to enable people to express their faith in and adoration of God and if leaders struggle to properly lead, it becomes a hindrance and you need to look at other ways to worship.

With the modern technology it is not difficult to have alternatives. With planning and using technology you can literally have the best worship music in the world while you worship and praise in your home. We often join with a local house church where they use technology in worship and it never fails to be powerful. With proper planning seeking the Lord the worship flows and as they worship there is an openness to listen to the Spirit and when needed to repeat a song with a quick push of a button. **The reason for this anointed worship is very simple: They pray and seek the Lord and come with a heart of worship and a desire to enter into the Lord's presence in worship and praise. That, more than anything else, will determine whether or not one enters into and experiences the presence of God.**

We have also been in house churches where a few instruments were used and without fail the presence of the Sprit has been tangible. One anointed leader with a simple instrument can open the door to the Holy of holies and the house can be filled with the powerful presence of the Lord. On other occasions we have been led through the veil by the singing of old-fashioned hymns with a leader using nothing but her voice and occasionally an African shaker to provide the rhythm. **Again, and again, the key is to come before the Lord with a heart open**

to worship and a hunger to enter into God's presence. It can happen as easily in a house setting as in a great auditorium.

We have found that both a meal at the table and worship allow children to join easily with adults. Worship and praise open the door for everyone to step into the presence of God and children move with ease into the place of intimacy, for it does not require rational understanding. The well-known story of Jesus cleansing the temple illustrates the point very well, for we read in Matthew 21:12-16:

> *Jesus entered the temple area and drove out all who were buying and selling there. He overturned the tables of the money changers and the benches of those selling doves. "It is written," he said to them, "'My house will be called a house of prayer,' but you are making it a 'den of robbers.'"*

> *The blind and the lame came to him at the temple, and he healed them. But when the chief priests and the teachers of the law saw the wonderful things he did and the children shouting in the temple area, "Hosanna to the Son of David," they were indignant.*

> *"Do you hear what these children are saying?" they asked him.*

> *"Yes," replied Jesus, "have you never read,*
> *"'From the lips of children and infants*
> *you have ordained praise'?"*

There are times when true worship is expressed in celebration with joy and shouts of praise. It is awesome to be together with other believers where this spontaneous joy erupts and where it is expressed. Children often pick this up better than adults and we have seen the power of worship expressed in shouts of praise amidst worship. It is powerful when children are free to celebrate and rejoice as they sense the powerful presence of Jesus.

Depending on the size of the meeting room in the house, flags and ribbons can add a special flavor to the celebration. These and small percussion instruments open the door to allow children to enter into worship and praise. Dancing also opens doors and is a great Scriptural way to worship and praise. Gathering in a home lends itself to such celebrations and for spontaneity in worship.

Worship and praise are closely tied to prayer and spiritual warfare. When Jesus cleansed the temple, he stated, "My father's house should be a house of prayer for all nations." Directly following this he healed many. This led to the children rejoicing and shouting praises in the temple that drew criticism from the chief priests and teachers of the law. Jesus responded by quoting Psalm 8. It is very interesting to read the quote in the context of Psalm 8:1-2:

O LORD, our Lord,
how majestic is your name in all the earth!

You have set your glory
above the heavens.
From the lips of children and infants
you have ordained praise because of your
enemies,
to silence the foe and the avenger.

The celebration of children in joy and praise silences the enemies of God. It shuts the mouth of the foe and the avenger. This type of worship is a powerful weapon against the enemy. Praise releases the wrath of God against the enemy as we read in Isaiah 30:27- 32:

See, the Name of the LORD comes from
afar,
with burning anger and dense clouds of
smoke;
his lips are full of wrath,
and his tongue is a consuming fire.
His breath is like a rushing torrent, rising
up to the neck.
He shakes the nations in the sieve of
destruction;
he places in the jaws of the peoples a bit that
leads them astray.
And you will sing
as on the night you celebrate a holy festival;
your hearts will rejoice

> *as when people go up with flutes to the*
> *mountain of the LORD,*
> *to the Rock of Israel.*
> *The LORD will cause men to hear his*
> *majestic voice*
> *and will make them see his arm coming*
> *down*
> *with raging anger and consuming fire,*
> *with cloudburst, thunderstorm and hail.*
> *The voice of the LORD will shatter Assyria;*
> *with his scepter he will strike them down.*
> *Every stroke the LORD lays on them*
> *with his punishing rod*
> *will be to the music of tambourines and*
> *harps,*
> *as he fights them in battle with the blows*
> *of his arm.*

Earlier we saw that Jesus overturned the tables and cleansed the temple, stating it was intended to be a house of prayer for all nations. When we gather as family of God in a house it provides many opportunities for prayer. In fact, one of the marks of the early church was their devotion to prayer (Acts 2:42). These gatherings for corporate prayer often took place in the homes as we read in Acts 4:23-31:

> *On their release, Peter and John went*
> *back to their own people and reported all*
> *that the chief priests and elders had said*
> *to them. When they heard this, they raised*
> *their voices together in prayer to God.*

"Sovereign Lord," they said, "you made the heaven and the earth and the sea, and everything in them. You spoke by the Holy Spirit through the mouth of your servant, our father David:

*"'Why do the nations rage
and the peoples plot in vain?
The kings of the earth take their stand
and the rulers gather together
against the Lord
and against his Anointed One.'*

Indeed, Herod and Pontius Pilate met together with the Gentiles and the people of Israel in this city to conspire against your holy servant Jesus, whom you anointed. They did what your power and will had decided beforehand should happen. Now, Lord, consider their threats and enable your servants to speak your word with great boldness. Stretch out your hand to heal and perform miraculous signs and wonders through the name of your holy servant Jesus."

<u>After they prayed, the place where they were meeting was shaken. And they were all filled with the Holy Spirit and spoke the word of God boldly.</u>

In Acts 12 Luke recorded the imprisonment of Peter after James had been executed. As the church prayed an angel literally helped Peter escape from prison and certain death. As the church recovers the power of prayer it has led to excitement and joy to join with others in corporate prayer. We see growing evidence of ordinary people stepping into the arena to pray with power and expectation. Far from being bored, children and youth often lead prayer and rejoice in opportunities to pray. Prayer and Spiritual warfare are important means to turn the hearts of the fathers to the children and the children to the fathers.

In practical terms we have had house church meetings where we started with worship and the presence of the Spirit just filled the place so that we spent time in the Holy of holies. Other times we started sharing (very much like the reporting of Peter and John in Acts 4) and as we were moved to pray, the risen Lord manifested in power just like the story in the book of Acts. **Worship, praise and prayer do not require big crowds and major buildings with sound systems and worship leaders – in fact all that are needed are hearts willing to seek and serve God.** When Jesus spoke to the Samaritan woman at the well, she questioned him about the place of worship in John 4:20-24:

> *"Our fathers worshiped on this mountain, but you Jews claim that the place where we must worship is in Jerusalem." Jesus declared, "Believe me, woman, <u>a time is coming when you will worship the Father</u>*

neither on this mountain nor in Jerusalem. You Samaritans worship what you do not know; we worship what we do know, for salvation is from the Jews. <u>Yet a time is coming and has now come when the true worshipers will worship the Father in spirit and truth, for they are the kind of worshipers the Father seeks. God is spirit, and his worshipers must worship in spirit and in truth.</u>"

With the right heart attitude, you and I can worship anywhere at any time with anyone sharing the same attitude and Spirit. Our homes are the ideal places to worship in Spirit and in truth and we see and experience that regularly! It is as simple as doing it!

Body Ministry

To me body ministry is one of the most exciting aspects of the house church model and no matter how we look at it, this is a vast change from the Levitical model used in our Western way of ministry. The small intimate setting of the house church is the only one that lends itself to a regular and consistent expression of the church as body where every member is an important part of the whole and where true body ministry can take place. The reason is very simple: As soon as a gathering includes more than a small number of members, some are overlooked and excluded in different ways.

In the intimate setting of the small gathering every member is important. Everyone has specific gifts from the Spirit given for the common good. This means that as we gather and someone shares a need, there will be an opportunity for one or more of the others to respond to the need and minister to the individual. As we minister using the gifts of the Spirit, we ourselves grow in faith and are build up and strengthened. In this way the whole body develops and grows.

How do we do this in practical terms? Again, there are different ways and approaches, but I will share what we often do. As we stated earlier, we prefer to meet around a table or in a social setting to begin. As we are together, we ask specific questions, e.g. what is happening in your life? Or, by simply looking at people through eyes of love, we will pick up specific needs or indications of needs. Once a need is identified, we invite response from others – giving opportunity for words of encouragement, prayer, wise counsel, etc. It is awesome to see how effective this is to break bondages and remove burdens from people's lives. We read in Isaiah 10:27:

> *It shall come to pass in that day*
> *That his burden will be taken away from*
> *your shoulder,*
> *And his yoke from your neck,*
> *And the yoke will be destroyed because of the*
> *anointing oil. NKJV*

Many of us who have been in charismatic circles are familiar with this verse from Scripture. Some time ago I was in a house church meeting and the leader made a very interesting observation. We often leave a meeting and say things like "there was a powerful anointing!" What we mean by that is that we sensed the presence of the Lord in a very tangible way. However, the true test of the anointing is not how we felt in the meeting, but whether those with burdens left without the heaviness and those under a heavy yoke of bondage walked out in freedom. That day every person left that particular house with burdens having been lifted and yokes broken. In fact, every time we are in this home, people leave without burdens or heavy yokes.

This happens because the anointing is not on one or two special individuals, but is on everyone. We read about this e.g. in 1 John 2:20:

> *But you have an anointing from the Holy One, and all of you know the truth.*

When we get together the anointing is released through each person to minister to one another. In fact, this is so important that we find it throughout the New Testament and to prove the point let us look at some Scriptures:

John 13:34-35:
> *"A new command I give you: <u>Love one another.</u> As I have loved you, so you must love one another. By this all men will know that you are my disciples, if you love one another."*

Romans 12:10-16:
> *<u>Be devoted to one another in brotherly love.</u> <u>Honor one another above yourselves.</u> Never be lacking in zeal, but keep your spiritual fervor, serving the Lord. Be joyful in hope, patient in affliction, faithful in prayer. Share with God's people who are in need. Practice hospitality.*

Bless those who persecute you; bless and do not curse. Rejoice with those who rejoice; mourn with those who mourn. <u>Live in harmony with one another.</u>

Romans 13:8-10:

<u>*Let no debt remain outstanding, except the continuing debt to love one another,*</u> *for he who loves his fellowman has fulfilled the law. The commandments, "Do not commit adultery," "Do not murder," "Do not steal," "Do not covet," and whatever other commandment there may be, are summed up in this one rule: "Love your neighbor as yourself." Love does no harm to its neighbor. Therefore, love is the fulfillment of the law.*

Romans 14:13:

Therefore, let us <u>stop passing judgment on one another.</u> Instead, make up your mind not to put any stumbling block or obstacle in your brother's way.

Romans 15:7:

<u>*Accept one another, then, just as Christ accepted you,*</u> *in order to bring praise to God.*

Romans 15:14:

I myself am convinced, my brothers, that you yourselves are full of goodness, complete in knowledge <u>and competent to instruct one another.</u>

1 Corinthians 1:10:

> *I appeal to you, brothers, in the name of our Lord Jesus Christ, <u>that all of you agree with one another</u> so that there may be no divisions among you and that you may be perfectly united in mind and thought.*

2 Corinthians 13:12:

> <u>*Greet one another with a holy kiss.*</u>

Galatians 5:13-15:

> *You, my brothers, were called to be free. But do not use your freedom to indulge the sinful nature; <u>rather, serve one another in love.</u> The entire law is summed up in a single command: "Love your neighbor as yourself." If you keep on biting and devouring each other, watch out or you will be destroyed by each other.*

Ephesians 4:1-6:

> *As a prisoner for the Lord, then, I urge you to live a life worthy of the calling you have received. <u>Be completely humble and gentle; be patient, bearing with one another in love. Make every effort to keep the unity of the Spirit through the bond of peace.</u> There is one body and one Spirit - just as you were called to one hope when you were called - one Lord, one faith, one baptism; one God and Father of all, who is over all and through all and in all.*

Ephesians 4:32:

> *Be kind and compassionate to one another,
> forgiving each other, just as in Christ God
> forgave you.*

Ephesians 5:15-21:

> *Be very careful, then, how you live-not as
> unwise but as wise, making the most of
> every opportunity, because the days are evil.
> Therefore, do not be foolish, but understand
> what the Lord's will is. Do not get drunk on
> wine, which leads to debauchery. Instead,
> be filled with the Spirit. Speak to one
> another with psalms, hymns and spiritual
> songs. Sing and make music in your heart to
> the Lord, always giving thanks to God the
> Father for everything, in the name of our
> Lord Jesus Christ.*

> *Submit to one another out of reverence for
> Christ.*

Colossians 3:12-17:

> *Therefore, as God's chosen people, holy
> and dearly loved, clothe yourselves with
> compassion, kindness, humility, gentleness
> and patience. Bear with each other and
> forgive whatever grievances you may have
> against one another. Forgive as the Lord
> forgave you. And over all these virtues put
> on love, which binds them all together in
> perfect unity.*

Let the peace of Christ rule in your hearts, since as members of one body you were called to peace. And be thankful. <u>Let the word of Christ dwell in you richly as you teach and admonish one another with all wisdom, and as you sing psalms, hymns and spiritual songs with gratitude in your hearts to God.</u> And whatever you do, whether in word or deed, do it all in the name of the Lord Jesus, giving thanks to God the Father through him.

1 Thessalonians 5:8-15:

But since we belong to the day, let us be self-controlled, putting on faith and love as a breastplate, and the hope of salvation as a helmet. For God did not appoint us to suffer wrath but to receive salvation through our Lord Jesus Christ. He died for us so that, whether we are awake or asleep, we may live together with him. <u>Therefore encourage one another and build each other up, just as in fact you are doing.</u>

Now we ask you, brothers, to respect those who work hard among you, who are over you in the Lord and who admonish you. Hold them in the highest regard in love because of their work. <u>Live in peace with each other.</u> And we urge you, brothers, warn those who are idle, encourage the timid, *help the weak, be patient with everyone. Make sure that nobody pays back wrong for wrong, <u>but always try to be kind to each other and to everyone else.</u>*

Hebrews 3:12-13:

See to it, brothers, that none of you has a sinful, unbelieving heart that turns away from the living God. <u>But encourage one another daily,</u> as long as it is called Today, so that none of you may be hardened by sin's deceitfulness.

Hebrews 10:23-25:

Let us hold unswervingly to the hope we profess, for he who promised is faithful. <u>And let us consider how we may spur one another on toward love and good deeds. Let us not give up meeting together, as some are in the habit of doing, but let us encourage one another - and all the more as you see the Day approaching.</u>

James 4:11:

<u>Brothers, do not slander one another.</u> Anyone who speaks against his brother or judges him speaks against the law and judges it.

1 Peter 1:22-23:

Now that you have purified yourselves by obeying the truth so that you have sincere *love for your brothers, <u>love one another deeply, from the heart.</u> For you have been born again, not of perishable seed, but of imperishable, through the living and enduring word of God.*

1 Peter 3:8-9:

> <u>*Finally, all of you, live in harmony with one another;*</u> *be sympathetic, love as brothers, be compassionate and humble. Do not repay evil with evil or insult with insult, but with blessing, because to this you were called so that you may inherit a blessing.*

1 Peter 4:7-11:

> *The end of all things is near. Therefore, be clear minded and self-controlled so that you can pray. <u>Above all, love each other deeply, because love covers over a multitude of sins. Offer hospitality to one another without grumbling. Each one should use whatever gift he has received to serve others, faithfully administering God's grace in its various forms.</u> If anyone speaks, he should do it as one speaking the very words of God. If anyone serves, he should do it with the strength God provides, so that in all things God may be praised through Jesus Christ. To him be the glory and the power for ever and ever. Amen.*

1 Peter 5:5:

Young men, in the same way be submissive to those who are older. <u>All of you, clothe yourselves with humility toward one another, because,</u>

"God opposes the proud,

But gives grace to the humble."

1 John 3:11:

This is the message you heard from the beginning: <u>We should love one another.</u>

1 John 4:7-12:

<u>Dear friends, let us love one another, for love comes from God.</u> Everyone who loves has been born of God and knows God. Whoever does not love does not know God, because God is love. This is how God showed his love among us: He sent his one and only Son into the world that we might live through him. This is love: not that we loved God, but that he loved us and sent his Son as an atoning sacrifice for our sins. Dear friends, since God so loved us, <u>we also ought to love one another. No one has ever seen God; but if we love one another, God lives in us and his love is made complete in us.</u>

2 John 5-6:

> *I ask that we love one another. And this is love: that we walk in obedience to his commands. As you have heard from the beginning, his command is that you walk in love.*

As we read these Scriptures the message is so simple! Ministry is to be body ministry and this happens when we get together in the small group. Over and over we find the words "one another" in these Scripture passages. **In contrast note that we never ever find any admonition like "Pastor, do this" or "Pastor, minister that!"** Ministry is designed to be members ministering to members and this works best and most effectively within a small group, because that allows everyone to be involved. The anointing is in every member and as we minister one to another the anointing flows to break the yokes of bondage and lift the burdens.

Body ministry also allows for the gifts in each person to be released as ordained by God. These gifts are given for ministry to the body as Paul wrote in 1 Corinthians12: 1-7:

> *Now about spiritual gifts, brothers, I do not want you to be ignorant. You know that when you were pagans, somehow or other you were influenced and led astray to mute idols. Therefore, I tell you that no one who is speaking by the Spirit of God says, "Jesus be cursed," and no one can say, "Jesus is Lord," except by the Holy Spirit.*

There are different kinds of gifts, but the same Spirit. There are different kinds of service, but the same Lord. There are different kinds of working, but the same God works all of them in all men.

<u>Now to each one the manifestation of the</u> <u>Spirit is given for the common good.</u>

Following this Paul explains how the gifts are to be used for this common good. We are each given gifts to minister to the other members. If anyone is hindered from exercising his or her gift or unwilling to do so, the whole body suffers. In practical terms the leaders of the meeting must be very discerning and encouraging the members to exercise their gifts. When we lead a meeting, it is an absolute joy to listen to the Spirit and help each member to join in ministry. When we minister to one person, as leader I am always inviting those led by the Spirit at that moment to come forward and share what they heard from the Lord. If there is no specific response, as leader I will listen to the Spirit and call specific people to join me in ministry. If they have not done this before, it is best to have them minister with a more seasoned person.

Some have been taught to fear possible transference of spirits from having some lay hands on them. Now, if someone is struggling in major areas of life, it is wise as leader to restrict some ministry and to keep an eye on them. However, the Holy Spirit is far more powerful than any demonic spirit and before ministry a specific prayer binding any demonic entity that might be present from interfering will be more than adequate in most cases. It is time we walk in victory and not in fear!

Most of the body needs will be met by the prayer and release of the gifts in ministry when the church gathers. Those with very specific needs e.g. healing from major abuse might require more intensive ministry. However, even they will grow and benefit from regular support and care from the members. Regular body ministry will take care of most every pastoral need that takes much of the time of "the Pastor" in traditional settings. In fact, body ministry eliminates most counseling needs. When such things in one member's life are dealt with in an intimate corporate setting in love, the other members often find answers to similar issues in their lives and are being built up at the same time. There needs to be wisdom and discernment practiced by the leader to keep confidential matters from becoming aired in public, but for most part most needs can be handled within the corporate body when gathered.

In and during ministry some may manifest. Depending on the members present there might be some who are not very comfortable with manifestations or some kinds of manifestations. It is very important to keep an eye on the members and deal with the issues of discomfort. For some manifestations may simply be new and thus bring discomfort. As leader one has to teach and explain how the presence of the Spirit can affect some people in specific ways. However, one needs to be aware that manifestations may also indicate the presence of demonic spirits, as we know from the ministry of Jesus. At times it is very obvious what the spirit is and it is easy to deal with the issue. When it is demonic, immediately take control and bind it and command it to be silent. Please note, authority in the Spirit does not depend on the loudness of one's voice! It is very much like teachers at school: The loudest ones are usually those who are insecure and try to intimidate with noise and threats. If you move in the Spirit you will walk in authority. When it begins to be a spectacle, it is out of order. Often it is best to simply bind the demonic spirit and set a time with the individual for deliverance.

When there is uncertainty about the spirit behind a manifestation, simply ask the Holy Spirit for discernment. As you meet regularly you will also get to know the various gifts operating through individual members. It is good to know who has the gift of discerning the spirits and at times all the leader will need is eye contact with such a person to confirm the origin of the spirit. Speaking of eye contact – this is also very important when discerning the spirit, as the eyes are the windows to the soul and when you look someone in the eye you will often know what spirit is in the person.

There are very important practical issues to keep in mind when ministry takes place. First and foremost, all ministry must flow from love. This means that the person who receives ministry must know and feel the love of those ministering. Jesus treated every person with love and even the woman caught in adultery knew he cared about her.

Thus no one must ever be made to feel embarrassed or ashamed during ministry. Care must at all times be taken to assure proper conduct and when dealing with issues of sexuality, no man (or men) should minister alone to a woman or vice versa. Wherever possible couples must be together in and during ministry, especially in a corporate setting. When hands are laid on someone for prayer it is very important that the touching is proper and cannot be misunderstood. People do fall on occasion while receiving ministry or prayer and it is good to train as many as possible how to catch such a person to prevent injury. Again, it is important to be very careful not to touch someone in the wrong way when catching! In ministry make sure that there is Kleenex available for times when tears flow. **These are just plain common-sense issues.**

Body ministry also includes the release of prophetic words. These words are to be expected when we meet together. In fact, prophetic words are to be encouraged and all should know that they are to seek the gift of prophecy as Paul wrote in 1 Corinthians 14:1-5:

> *<u>Follow the way of love and eagerly desire spiritual gifts, especially the gift of prophecy.</u> For anyone who speaks in a tongue does not speak to men but to God. Indeed, no one understands him; he utters mysteries with his spirit. <u>But everyone who prophesies speaks to men for their strengthening, encouragement and comfort.</u> He who speaks in a tongue edifies himself, but <u>he</u>*

> *who prophesies edifies the church. I would*
> *like every one of you to speak in tongues, but*
> *I would rather have you prophesy. He who*
> *prophesies is greater than one who speaks*
> *in tongues, unless he interprets, so that the*
> *church may be edified.*

As stated above, these words of prophecy should be expected when God's people meet. Note that this gift is not difficult to release. It flows from love like every gift. **This is how prophecy operates in the body. When I look at someone through the eyes of love as Jesus did, I will see not just the needs, which call for ministry and pastoral care. When I look at someone in love, I ask the Spirit to let me see God's word that will encourage, strengthen and comfort that person. That word is prophetic! The same applies to a group like a house church. As I look at the group, I ask God for his word for them. That is what prophecy is all about. The idea is to hear God's word that will edify and build the individual or the group up.** This is not only applicable to prophecy, but also to the other gifts as we read in 1 Corinthians 14:26:

> *What then shall we say, brothers? When you*
> *come together, everyone has a hymn, or a*
> *word of instruction, a revelation, a tongue*
> *or an interpretation. All of these must be*
> *done for the strengthening of the church.*

Let us put this in perspective in the context of the church meeting in a house. Where two or three are

gathered in Jesus' name he manifests as risen Lord. One of the ways he does this is by being who he is as head of his body, the church. As head he directs the members through the Spirit to minister to one another's needs. He does this by releasing the gifts of the Spirit to build up his body. Thus, when one member has a specific need, through the Spirit someone speaks a prophetic word of encouragement, another shares a word of Scripture, another prays in the Spirit and someone interprets the word, another lays hands on the person and prays for healing and restoration. Leadership is simply to guide and direct the release of the gifts encouraging everyone to be involved, for we all need one another. As we do the risen Jesus works in and through us to build his body. His anointing in each of us touches each member and yokes are broken and burdens lifted. This is why house churches that function properly are healthy and strong and pastoral care is not a burden to the leadership.

Before we move to the next chapter, I need to make a few more observations about the order of the meetings. **There is a freedom in the Spirit, but also order.** We find direction for keeping order in 1 Corinthians 14:27-33 and 39-40:

> *If anyone speaks in a tongue, two-or at the most three-should speak, one at a time, and someone must interpret. If there is no interpreter, the speaker should keep quiet in the church and speak to himself and God.*

Two or three prophets should speak, and the others should weigh carefully what is said. And if a revelation comes to someone who is sitting down, the first speaker should stop. For you can all prophesy in turn so that everyone may be instructed and encouraged. <u>The spirits of prophets are subject to the control of prophets.</u> For God is not a God of disorder but of peace.

Therefore, my brothers, be eager to prophesy, and do not forbid speaking in tongues. But everything should be done in a fitting and orderly way.

These are very easy to understand and I do not need to explain anything. There is one key observation that we need to see, though. When a prophetic word or revelation comes to someone, it does not have to be spoken forth at that moment. In fact, many times what is spoken out prophetically was never intended to be released. Much of what is spoken forth as prophecy is often revelation for us to enable us to intercede for the other person. It is not through the gift of prophesy, but through the gift of discernment! Thus, when prophetic revelation comes to me, the first thing to do is to ask the Spirit what I am to do with the revelation. Most of what God reveals to us is for the prayer closet and only for the prayer closet. Those who truly seek God's revelation and treasure what he reveals rarely speak the words forth, for they know how to keep confidence. We read this in Psalm 25:12-14:

Who, then, is the man that fears the LORD?
He will instruct him in the way chosen
for him.
He will spend his days in prosperity,
and his descendants will inherit the land.
The LORD confides in those who fear him;
he makes his covenant known to them.

Those that know how to keep confidence and who treasure the revelation of God find that he reveals his secrets to them. They know to seek him and will not speak it forth unless the Spirit releases them to do this. They pray through the prophetic revelation and intercede for those in need as the Spirit reveals the secrets. As a result, they are more effective in prayer than most, for they pray with Spiritual insight according to the heart of God. Those who do not understand this have identified it as "the gift of intercession" for they have seen the heart of prayer and the power released as these people pray. Many who hear from the Lord never stop to seek him regarding the revelation and simply speak the words forth and break the confidence. Much of what goes forth as prophecy is abuse of God's revelation and God will not keep revealing his secrets if we do not keep confidence. The prophetic word and the spirits of prophecy are truly under the control of the prophets. The verbal diarrhea that is rampant in churches and prophetic circles is out of line with the word of God. The teaching that whatever I hear or see is to be spoken out is wrong.

Another thing to note is that the prophetic word is to be weighed or judged. This is to be done as Paul said "by the others." In most churches where the gifts of the Spirit are released there are rules regarding the release of prophetic words. As these churches function with Levitical power structures, the rules are set up to have appointed leaders or the pastor judge the word – often forcing the speaker to first submit it for approval before it is spoken forth. However, as we know the New Testament church never functioned as a Levitical structure and the words in 1 Corinthians 14:29 in the context simply says that the prophetic words should be spoken one at a time so that everyone in the house can hear and the other members of the body present, having heard the word, are to judge it. It has nothing to do with the control issues in the current church where only those words that the leadership approves may be spoke forth.

Ministry is for the body of believers and is to be done by the members according to their gifts to build one another up and to strengthen the body. It was never intended as a specialized function of a chosen few ordained to do ministry on behalf of the body. This works best in a small setting and this is why the church meets in houses. The real exciting thing is that as members minister in this way, each one is built up and strengthened. Each one has a place and a special function and servant hood is practiced every time the church gathers. Advice and encouragement are shared and testimonies are heard, for as each one grows, they become confident and equipped to minister outside in the world. They interact with the world and touch and transform lives. Ordinary people become extraordinary royal priests and begin to pray for unbelievers who have needs. They invite others to come and meet Jesus in their home and evangelism happens as result. Roger, one of the house church leaders walking in relationship with us watched as a Moslem immigrant was treated badly by a supervisor at work. A gentle word of encouragement in a tough work environment opened the door for this man and his wife to come to Roger's home for counseling just before Christmas. Later this Moslem family gave a Christmas gift to Roger and his wife, Ginette. Doors are opening as a result. An ordinary machinist is touching lives in the workplace and his home is the place where a vibrant church meets and lives are changed. This is the Third Day Church rising up and the light beginning to shine in the dark!

We can continue to talk about body ministry, but it is time to move on to the touchy subject of money.

Offerings and Financial Matters

For those coming out of the Levitical system of the contemporary church with the emphasis on buildings, programs and salaries for clergy and staff members this will be a big paradigm shift. To begin let us read Romans 12:1-2:

> *Therefore, I urge you, brothers, in view of God's mercy, to offer your bodies as living sacrifices, holy and pleasing to God-this is your spiritual act of worship. <u>Do not conform any longer to the pattern of this world, but be transformed by the renewing of your mind.</u> Then you will be able to test and approve what God's will is - his good, pleasing and perfect will.*

The Levitical system is nothing else than the system of this world. As we move to the way the Kingdom is to function, we find it can only come about through a radical renewing of our minds. This mindset will lead to the Kingdom lifestyle and prove that the King's will is good, pleasing and perfect. I have discussed this in detail in other books, but **the key principle is that a true Kingdom vision flows from the recognition that everything we have belongs to the King of kings. We are simply stewards and are accountable to him for the way in which we use every resource entrusted to us. The Old Testament Levitical model is based on a tithe while the New Testament Kingdom model is based on giving it all to God. It is not 10%, but 100%. Until we settle the issue of control over resources and submit it all to him, we will not walk in the Kingdom vision.**

Having said that, it is time to move on to the great news of Kingdom finances. God's design of the house as the primary meeting place in which the gifts are released for body ministry has major financial implications. **The costly overhead of the church structure that we know is not necessary at all! There is no major expense when we meet in homes and the members exercise their gifts thus eliminating the cost of programs and paid professionals (otherwise known as pastors and staff members). This means we are free to use the resources given by God to meet real needs. We can actually act like "the Good Samaritan" and be a neighbor for the person in need. We can choose to meet Jesus in the person in need as pictured in Matthew 25. We do not have to be forced into being goats by a church system where "leaders" allocate the resources according to the budget designed to support the Levitical system, which Jesus abolished when he died on the cross!**

So, we do not have to live under the law of tithes and offerings to support the Levites and their temples where they run the programs that they design to keep the system going. Instead of a measly 10% we are now free to give 100% and live as the children of the King. Instead of the leaders drawing up the budget to maintain the buildings, run programs and pay staff (and bury the talents of the body in the pews), we are set free to give as the Spirit guides us. As Paul wrote in 2 Corinthians 9:6-11:

> *Remember this: Whoever sows sparingly will also reap sparingly, and whoever sows generously will also reap generously. Each man should give what he has decided in his heart to give, not reluctantly or under compulsion, for God loves a cheerful giver. And God is able to make all grace abound to you, so that in all things at all times, having all that you need, you will abound in every good work. As it is written:*

> *"He has scattered abroad his gifts to the poor; his righteousness endures forever."*

> *Now he who supplies seed to the sower and bread for food will also supply and increase your store of seed and will enlarge the harvest of your righteousness. You will be made rich in every way so that you can be generous on every occasion, and through us your generosity will result in thanksgiving to God.*

Listen carefully so you do not miss the point: Settle the issue of possessions up front and place all you have and ever will have on the altar and walk away. The Kingdom model is demonstrated in Jesus' challenge to the rich young ruler. This is why Paul wrote in 1 Timothy 6:6-10:

> *But godliness with contentment is great gain. <u>For we brought nothing into the world, and we can take nothing out of it.</u> But if we have food and clothing, we will be content with that. People who want to get rich fall into temptation and a trap and into many foolish and harmful desires that plunge men into ruin and destruction. <u>For the love of money is a root of all kinds of evil. Some people, eager for money, have wandered from the faith and pierced themselves with many griefs.</u>*

Once you have settled the issue of possessions, learn to handle that which is entrusted to you with a true Kingdom mindset. Learn to be generous, but be a good steward of the King's resources. Seek the guidance of the Spirit as you give and make sure you invest in the Kingdom of God and not in someone's kingdom, however well intentioned.

The wonderful thing about the house churches is that there is no overhead. This leaves the resources from being wasted and those giving can direct the gifts to where there is real need. There is a warning in this though: As you move into the freedom of being generous with your resources you will be put to the test. Many of us having been used to the Western church system have gotten accustomed to avoid dealing with the Lord when he shows up in the person in need. It is easy to refer the person to the pastor or to the benevolence committee when they need help and walk away feeling good. In the Third Day Church we cannot hide behind someone else or behind the structure. We have to face issues head on. If a brother or sister is in need, I cannot simply pray and walk away, as we read in James 2:14-18:

> *What good is it, my brothers, if a man claims to have faith but has no deeds? Can such faith save him? Suppose a brother or sister is without clothes and daily food. If one of you says to him, "Go, I wish you well; keep warm and well fed," but does nothing about his physical needs, what good is it? In the same way, faith by itself, if it is not accompanied by action, is dead.*

> *But someone will say, "You have faith; I have deeds."*

> *Show me your faith without deeds, and I will show you my faith by what I do.*

So how do we handle offerings in a house church setting? There is more than one way to approach this. Within North America most are used to receiving tax receipts when giving to charitable organizations. There are pros and cons to this and I do not wish to debate these here. The fact is that not every house church will be registered as a charitable organization. Some that I know are and they can thus issue such receipts. Those who are not can handle this by formally joining an existing network with charitable status and work through the other organization. **It is very important in such matters to get legal advice to ensure that you operate within the law.** Some choose to simply operate in faith without the charitable status and they keep books and members will disburse income according to the needs they see. Some choose not to take offerings at all, but encourage members to give where and when prompted by the Spirit, whether to charities or to individual needs they encounter. **Whatever you choose, make sure that you heard from the Spirit and that you operate legally.**

As I see the Third Day Church arising, more and more house churches will be birthed. These churches will interconnect to form networks with others. Itinerant ministers functioning in the five-fold gifts will relate to these churches and the churches with them. In contrast to the present-day denominational structures where certain churches belong to a certain "denomination", the networks will be less formal. Some of the house churches will use their offerings to support one or more of these networks as the Spirit leads them. Within this model those who do not have charitable status will direct giving towards specific apostolic networks, very much like the early church where members laid their offerings at the feet of the apostles as we read in Acts 4:32-37:

All the believers were one in heart and mind. No one claimed that any of his possessions was his own, but they shared everything they had. With great power the apostles continued to testify to the resurrection of the Lord Jesus, and much grace was upon them all. There were no needy persons among them. For from time to time those who owned lands or houses sold them, brought the money from the sales and put it at the apostles' feet, and it was distributed to anyone as he had need.

Joseph, a Levite from Cyprus, whom the apostles called Barnabas (which means Son of Encouragement), sold a field he owned and brought the money and put it at the apostles' feet.

Through true apostolic networks specific needs will be met as people give. Sometimes the giving will be directed to appeals to meet specific needs, very much like the collection that was taken throughout the early church to help the church in Jerusalem during the time of the famine as we read in Acts 11:27-30:

During this time some prophets came down from Jerusalem to Antioch. One of them, named Agabus, stood up and through the Spirit predicted that a severe famine would spread over the entire Roman world. (This happened during the reign of Claudius.)

*The disciples, each according to his ability,
decided to provide help for the brothers
living in Judea. This they did, sending their
gift to the elders by Barnabas and Saul.*

The support money was collected in a systematic way and delivered to those in need by Paul and his companions. **It is very important to note that these gifts were given to deal with specific needs related to people. What was entrusted to the apostles were to be used to feed the hungry and meet the needs of the poor. These funds were not to buy "church properties" or for programs, as we are used to in the Western church. Nor were they for salaries for resident clergy "doing the ministry." There were no resident clergy, for the ministry was released to the body. The itinerant leaders did receive support as we will discuss later. Please note that the gifts were voluntary as the Spirit led each member of the body to give.** We read this in 2 Corinthians 9:7 where Paul wrote to them to be ready with the gift when Titus would arrive to receive it and said:

*Each man should give what he has decided
in his heart to give, not reluctantly or under
compulsion, for God loves a cheerful giver.*

There is ample evidence in Scripture that the itinerant ministers received support from the churches when they were visiting and ministering. Paul wrote that this was to be expected, although he personally chose not to exercise that right himself, as we read in 1 Corinthians 9:1-15:

Am I not free? Am I not an apostle? Have I not seen Jesus our Lord? Are you not the result of my work in the Lord? Even though I may not be an apostle to others, surely, I am to you! For you are the seal of my apostleship in the Lord.

This is my defense to those who sit in judgment on me. Don't we have the right to food and drink? Don't we have the right to take a believing wife along with us, as do the other apostles and the Lord's brothers and Cephas? Or is it only I and Barnabas who must work for a living?

Who serves as a soldier at his own expense? Who plants a vineyard and does not eat of its grapes? Who tends a flock and does not drink of the milk? Do I say this merely from a human point of view? Doesn't the Law say the same thing? For it is written in the Law of Moses: "Do not muzzle an ox while it is treading out the grain." Is it about oxen that God is concerned? Surely, he says this for us, doesn't he? Yes, this was written for us, because when the plowman plows and the thresher threshes, they ought to do so in the hope of sharing in the harvest. If we have sown spiritual seed among you, is it too much if we reap a material harvest from you? If others have this right of support from you, shouldn't we have it all the more?

But we did not use this right. On the contrary, we put up with anything rather than hinder the gospel of Christ. Don't you know that those who work in the temple get their food from the temple, and those who serve at the altar share in what is offered on the altar? <u>In the same way, the Lord has commanded that those who preach the gospel should receive their living from the gospel. But I have not used any of these rights.</u>

It is very important to note the following: **The itinerant leaders and those traveling with them received support, but they did not enforce that.** The support was to come as the Spirit prompted the members. Some churches chose to support specific leaders more than others, e.g. the church in Philippi supported Paul's ministry in many ways as we read in Philippians 1:3-6 and 4:14-19:

I thank my God every time I remember you. In all my prayers for all of you, I always pray with joy because of your partnership in the gospel from the first day until now, being confident of this, that he who began a good work in you will carry it on to completion until the day of Christ Jesus.

Yet it was good of you to share in my troubles. Moreover, as you Philippians know, in the early days of your acquaintance with the gospel, when I set out from Macedonia, not one church shared with me in the matter of giving and receiving, except you only; for even when I was in Thessalonica, you sent me aid again and again when I was in need. Not that I am looking for a gift, but I am looking for what may be credited to your account. I have received full payment and even more; I am amply supplied, now that I have received from Epaphroditus the gifts you sent. They are a fragrant offering, an acceptable sacrifice, pleasing to God. And my God will meet all your needs according to his glorious riches in Christ Jesus.

In practical terms today we see how those functioning in the five-fold ministry are supported through voluntary gifts to cover personal and ministry needs. The key issue is that these gifts are voluntary gifts and flow from relationship established as the leaders equip the saints for their work of ministry. In addition to these personal gifts, there are times when specific gifts are given to such itinerant leaders to meet specific needs, as illustrated in the Biblical example of the special offering for the church in Jerusalem above.

Our personal teaching is simple: We are called to encourage and work alongside the home churches by equipping the saints for their work of ministry. We have a specific call to equip and release leaders. We do not expect any financial reward and we do not lay down conditions about financial support for our ministry. We trust the Holy Spirit as he speaks to the individual churches and leaders. We have seen the results and recognize that the Spirit works in different ways. The Spirit led one house church to draw up a covenant where they committed to walk in covenant relationship with us for a season and they committed to give a tithe of their church's offerings to support our ministry at the time. Others choose to give love offerings and we have had from modest to extravagant gifts. We have also been privileged to minister as a gift to others with no financial reward. We have never felt comfortable with expecting and demanding specific "rates" for the ministry we do. It is not in Scripture and no matter how well we try to argue for this approach, it falls short. There are practical issues to consider, e.g. travel costs, meals, etc. However, if it is God's call, he will provide. The key is to listen to the Spirit and trust God for the provision.

We do recognize that as the Third Day Church arises there will be more house churches and the networks will grow bigger. Most emerging networks will provide structures for the churches that choose to walk in relationship and do not have charitable status to channel offerings through the networks in legal ways. There are already some models that could be applied or modified. However, the key issue is to recognize this and work within the laws of the land.

As we discuss these issues it is very important to be discerning and wise when entering into relationships where funds are handled through another organization. Much of what is currently happening in "apostolic networks" is simply no different than the worldly denominational structures of control, where you pay your membership fee to belong! This is where the unholy and un-Biblical idea of "covering" has been so often misused. What we propose is very different and flows from a different heart. We talk about house churches where the networking is through relationship and mutual submission, without financial controls over the funds by those with whom they choose to network. **I have the full confidence that the Holy Spirit is fully capable to direct the members of the body on every issue including how to handle the resources entrusted to their care – individually and corporately! The ones who find this the most difficult are those with a vested interest in controlling the money for their own purposes.**

As the true apostolic networks develop there will be support for the wider network and the wider ministry through these networks. However, the foundation of the networks must be based on true relationship and support should be voluntary as the Spirit leads. Much of this wider support will come through offerings at joint gatherings like celebrations where house churches gather together for worship and praise. Support will also come through special offerings in house churches when itinerant leaders visit and minister, very much like the New Testament picture. On other occasions special gifts will be sent from house churches to specific leaders and networks with which they have relationships.

With that said, it is time to take a closer look at the emerging networks and how they function.

Networking with One Another

Let us begin by stating the New Testament picture very clearly. Every house church is a full church. It is to function fully as the church. It is not a cell of a larger unit called the church. At the same time, there is to be an inter-dependence and networking between these churches in the unity of the Spirit. The networking is facilitated by those called to the fivefold ministry, just like Paul networked the churches through his letters, and by the visits of apostolic leaders as well as believers to different churches.

The basis of the networking is the unity we have in Christ Jesus. This unity is to be expressed and is vital for the world to witness as Jesus prayed in John 17:20-23:

> *My prayer is not for them alone. I pray also for those who will believe in me through their message, that all of them may be one, Father, just as you are in me and I am in you. May they also be in us so that the world may believe that you have sent me. I have*

given them the glory that you gave me, that they may be one as we are one: I in them and you in me. May they be brought to complete unity to let the world know that you sent me and have loved them even as you have loved me.

This unity is in the Spirit and one of the best ways to express it is when the different churches gather together for a celebration of worship or for prayer. This is the essence of the words in Ephesians 4:1-6:

As a prisoner for the Lord, then, I urge you to live a life worthy of the calling you have received. Be completely humble and gentle; be patient, bearing with one another in love. <u>Make every effort to keep the unity of the Spirit through the bond of peace.</u> There is one body and one Spirit - just as you were called to one hope when you were called - one Lord, one faith, one baptism; one God and Father of all, who is over all and through all and in all.

It is very important to see that this unity is in the Spirit through the bond of peace. Listen again to that: it is not through submission to "a covering body" or through doctrinal agreement or through leaders getting together and inviting others to join them. It is all God's people getting together with one another in humility and expressing the unity in our Lord. This is why the current moves to unity based on the Levitical leadership of

Western churches getting together to express unity and draw the body into unity will not work. The idea is good, but the very issue of Levitical leadership is the cause of the biggest division in the church today, that is the division between "clergy" and "laity." The unity in the Spirit is when the churches simply join together with others to express the unity of the body.

How does this work in practical terms? At present we are in the very foundational stages of the Third Day Church rising up. However, the unity of the body is easily expressed as local house churches join with others in larger gatherings for celebrations. We have held such celebrations with local house churches on a regular basis. For the celebrations we rented the facilities of a church in the community on a Saturday night when it is normally available. In practical terms doing it in this way means we have the access to a sound system and to everything we need to host a celebration at a minimal cost - and in the process this local church is blessed financially. A freewill offering easily covers the cost. Such gatherings allow the members to enter into forms and expressions of worship that are often not possible in the smaller house church settings. There is also cross-pollination as testimonies are shared and as members from one church minister to members from another church.

The celebrations usually look like "worship service in church," but there are major differences. First those coming are coming not just as individuals, but also as members of a local church. They regularly receive personal body ministry and there is less pressure and need for individual ministry at the celebrations. Coming from local churches where they are actively involved in ministry there are also no pent-up frustrations with gifts that had been stifled (buried in pews by leaders) and there is more peace than in regular church services. When it comes to ministry times, we seek the Spirit as to who are to pray and do ministry. There is never a lack of experienced leaders to do ministry and it opens the door for those in attendance to receive ministry from someone other than their own local church. It is amazing to see the variety in the Lord's body when local churches gather. One church will have a special anointing in worship, another in evangelism, and another in pastoral care, etc. As they share testimonies of what God is doing in their community these anointings and gifts become very transparent. When it comes to ministry time someone from one church can tap into the anointing from a different church and have that gift stirred up by receiving ministry from the other church team. This is where the cross-pollination happens. There is also no need for a leader to preach a sermon – simply time to worship, praise and share!

Such contacts also open the door to further cross-pollination as relationships are built and invitations extended for some from one church to minister in another church. It further opens doors for specific help when needed in certain areas, e.g. when there is a specific counseling need that our church cannot meet, we have access to others with the gifts needed and we can refer the person in need or when necessary accompany him or her to the person who can help. One of the main functions of such celebrations is to facilitate the establishment of relationships between members and leaders from different churches. Within the Third Day Church networking functions on different levels and it is relationship based. It is less formal and yet much stronger and far more effective. We have found that it is very helpful to have a time of fellowship prior to the celebration. It is no problem to have some juice and cookies available for the people as they come and this allows an opportunity to introduce new members or new church leaders to others in a relaxed and informal setting. This has the further advantage that it cuts down on the number of latecomers at the celebration and eases the burden at the end of the service.

Another level of networking arises out of the relationships between churches and leaders with those operating in the fivefold ministry. Note that this also flows out of relationship. The foundations of the celebrations are apostolic in nature. As the Third Day Church arises there will be increasing numbers of such networks with apostolic leaders and teams working in fellowship to train and equip members for the work of ministry.

It is very important to understand how the fivefold ministry will function in the Third Day Church. **The fivefold ministry is by nature itinerant.** Apostles and prophets planting a church may for a season lead that church and equip the members, but if they stay to "pastor" the church it is wrong! The key issue for the apostles and prophets is to lay basic foundations and equip and release the people in ministry. They are to discern when it is time to release the church to function on its own. In the process they build relationships with the people and leaders for the future networking and equipping. As they do this they work with others like pastors, teachers and evangelists and network them with the local churches to equip and strengthen these churches.

In the current North American society, there are more and more gifted and trained people moving out of the Levitical structures of our churches. They are responding to the call of the Spirit, often without realizing that. They have walked through the gates of control and into the desert of the world, whether as conscious choice or simply because they could not take it inside the walls anymore. As a result, there are many wandering outside in the world like sheep without a shepherd. A large number are people with strong leadership skills, called and even equipped to do the work of ministry, but they were never released. These people have been wounded and hurt by the Levitical leaders and structures. They just need a little guidance and encouragement with an apostolic leader coming beside them for a season to restore and release them into ministry. It is no different than in Jesus' day as we read in Matthew 9:35-38:

> *Jesus went through all the towns and villages, teaching in their synagogues, preaching the good news of the kingdom and healing every disease and sickness. When he saw the crowds, he had compassion on them,*

because they were harassed and helpless, like sheep without a shepherd. Then he said to his disciples, "The harvest is plentiful but the workers are few. Ask the Lord of the harvest, therefore, to send out workers into his harvest field."

The fields are ripe and the harvest is plentiful. As the apostolic teams arise so will the Third Day Church arise and shine. Currently we have exciting opportunities and the potential is awesome for the house churches to be established. In fact, many are already in existence and functioning, but because of the North American mindset many involved do not even recognize what is happening. In a real way the truth has been hidden because of the mindset that the church is a building and needs programs. The apostle Paul as Jew found the revelation of the mystery of the gospel and that the Gentiles were included in Christ. As that was a revelation to Paul, today for many believers it is also the revelation of a mystery that they can experience the presence of the risen Lord outside of the church building when they meet in a local home and that the very power that raised Jesus from the dead is available to them. However, once they get this revelation, they are ready to be the church, meet as body and network with apostolic leaders and other churches.

The process of this Third Day Church rising up has begun. It is small and therefore many have not even noticed it yet, but within a very short time it will be very noticeable. The major networking is coming as it should by divine appointment as people are drawn by the Spirit to connect with those with a like mind and heart. At present the Spirit is bringing together potential leaders of house churches with the no-name apostles and prophets. We do not have to seek for people. They come and find us. The Spirit is also beginning to stir in these leaders to develop the resources and working models of this Third Day Church. We are now in a position to get the message out and many who hear this message find that it "strangely warms their hearts" and they receive it with joy. We find that some current house churches are already functioning well, but they never realized that they actually are the church! Many who have moved out of the Levitical system simply meet together, fellowship and minister to one another, but they never connected the dots to see that they are in fact the church at someone's house! When they connect with apostolic people and leaders the picture comes into focus and they thrive with the support and blessing of the emerging networks.

We read in Luke 10:1-7:

> *After this the Lord appointed seventy-two others and sent them two by two ahead of him to every town and place where he was about to go. He told them, "The harvest is plentiful, but the workers are few. Ask the Lord of the harvest, therefore, to send out workers into his harvest field. Go! I am sending you out like lambs among wolves.*

Do not take a purse or bag or sandals; and do not greet anyone on the road.

<u>*When you enter a house, first say, 'Peace to this house.' If a man of peace is there, your peace will rest on him; if not, it will return to you. Stay in that house, eating and drinking whatever they give you, for the worker deserves his wages. Do not move around from house to house."*</u>

Today there are many houses where there are men and women of peace ready to receive the itinerant ministries of the emerging Third Day Church. Some we need to find through divine guidance and revelation, as Paul and his companions were led to Europe and met Lydia who opened her house. Others will find us through divine guidance, like Cornelius who found Peter through the vision recorded in Acts 10.

There is another important issue to notice and it is in the passage quoted above: The workers responding to the Spirit to enter into this harvest field are sent like lambs among wolves. Many in the church speak about a coming persecution and they are right on. However, most foresee this coming persecution as a curtailing of the "rights" of the church in this Western society with its increasing secularism and growing hostility towards the church. There will be changes and opposition in this way, **but the real persecution will come from the established church and its Levitical leadership just as it did in the days when the First Day Church rose up!** The issue is simple: It is a matter of control over the resources entrusted to God's people. The Levitical structures need major financial support and those who will be affected the most are those on top of the hierarchical structures, the paid staff members! Do not be surprised if you are asked who gave you the authority to do what you are doing (they asked this of Jesus and of his followers!) and make sure you do not become a wolf yourself. Remember that when the Lamb of God was led to be killed *"as a sheep before her shearers is silent, <u>so he did not open his mouth.</u>"* Isaiah 53:7.

At the present moment there is little opposition to the house church movement for many have not even noticed. Some have sensed the Spirit moving in this direction and are actively seeking to express this within the Levitical system through cell-structures. This will not work as it is trying to patch the old garment by snipping up the new one! To those who are in true house churches: Enjoy the freedom, but expect the opposition as the networks begin to gain in numbers and strength. More importantly, focus on the task at hand and do the work of ministry as the Spirit leads you. Personally, I have found that as I have more than enough to do positively, I have no time to end up in endless disputes with the leaders of the accepted Western model. Again, I have full confidence that the Holy Spirit is far better than I am at revealing the truth to people and all I need is to be obedient and work with those who are open and willing to work with me. As the early church moved out, they were bold in their witness and when needed spoke with great boldness to the Jewish hierarchy, but never compromised as we read e.g. in Acts 4:18-20:

> *Then they called them in again and commanded them not to speak or teach at all in the name of Jesus. But Peter and John replied, "Judge for yourselves whether it is right in God's sight to obey you rather than God. For we cannot help speaking about what we have seen and heard."*

As the story unfolded the church grew and in Acts 6:7 we read that *"the number of disciples in Jerusalem increased rapidly, and a large number of priests became obedient to the faith."*

Ultimate it is not you or I that will build the church. When Peter made the great statement of faith that Jesus is the Messiah, the Son of God, we read in Matthew 16:17-19:

> *Jesus replied, "Blessed are you, Simon son of Jonah, for this was not revealed to you by man, but by my Father in heaven. And I tell you that you are Peter, and on this rock I <u>will build my church, and the gates of Hades will not overcome it.</u> I will give you the keys of the kingdom of heaven; whatever you bind on earth will be bound in heaven, and whatever you loose on earth will be loosed in heaven."*

Jesus himself will build his church. It is not through power or might, but through his Spirit. **All we need to do is to be obedient to the call on our lives and in obedience open our homes and be the church, ministering to one another and to the world and encouraging one another to grow in faith, witness and understanding. Be open to the guidance of the Spirit and network with others as you keep the unity of the Spirit through the bond of peace. As you do this, you will meet new kinds of leaders, coming as gifts from the Lord – serving as apostles, prophets, evangelists, pastors and teachers to equip and release the members of the body for their work of ministry. You will know them by the fruit they produce that will be visible in the lives of those they serve. They will not come with titles or demands, but with a humble spirit and they will move in power. They will be there to encourage, equip and release people and will often come in teams and will build kingdom networks.**

These networks will more than often be very informal and will always be rooted and grounded in relationship that comes through service. Rather than demanding loyalty and expecting submission, the true five-fold leaders will walk as servants and their walk will command respect. They will stress mutual submission and will be known as encouragers. They will not only walk in relationship with house churches, but also in relationship with one another.

For the most part these leaders will be No-names. It is only as you get to know them and work with them that you will see their gift. As you receive them, you will be blessed and you will receive the very gift they are, as Jesus for example said in Matthew 10:40-42:

> *"He who receives you receives me, and he who receives me receives the one who sent me. Anyone who receives a prophet because he is a prophet will receive a prophet's reward, and anyone who receives a righteous man because he is a righteous man will receive a righteous man's reward. And if anyone gives even a cup of cold water to one of these little ones because he is my disciple, I tell you the truth, he will certainly not lose his reward."*

As you open the door of your house for Jesus and the members of his body to enter in, there are many rewards that will come through the door. This is what the Third Day Church network is all about. It is Jesus building his church through servant leaders equipping the saints for the work of ministry, so that the body of Christ may be built up until we all reach unity in the faith and in the knowledge of the Son of God and become mature, attaining to the whole measure of the fullness of Christ. Then we will no longer be infants, tossed back and forth by the waves, and blown here and there by every wind of teaching and by the cunning and craftiness of men in their deceitful scheming. Instead, speaking the truth in love, we will in all things grow up into him who is the Head, that is, Christ. From him the whole body, joined and held together by every supporting ligament, grows and builds itself up in love, as each part does its work (Ephesians 4:11-16).

On this Third Day he is perfecting his body and he is pouring the new wine that will not be held in the old wineskins – and as we open the door of our homes, he will enter in and have communion with us. In this simple and easy process, ordinary people like you and I are equipped and released to be extraordinary royal priests and the glory of the Lord fills our homes. In the process the cry of creation for the revelation of the sons of God is being answered (Romans 8:19) and the words of the prophet in Habakkuk 2:14 is set in motion as the glory of God flows from our homes through our neighborhoods to connect with other homes for ultimately the earth will be filled with the knowledge of the glory of the LORD, as the waters cover the sea.

It is as easy as opening your home and meeting with people – keeping some practical issues in mind, including legal matters. To these we need to turn next.

Legal Matters for House Churches

As we move to the establishment of house churches and networks there are some legal matters to keep in mind, especially within this litigious society. I will only touch on the issues, as I am not in any way competent to deal with these matters in any detail, but will simply point to potential things to keep in mind.

First there are local municipal bylaws that one has to keep in mind. Most of these are simple common-sense things and should not be a hindrance. In our culture with many traveling in vehicles to meetings, the availability of parking could present potential problems. It is vital that the needs of neighbors be taken into account, e.g. by not blocking driveways or ignoring no parking signs. In addition to parking, meetings should not cause a disturbance in any way. Loud worship in one house may not at all affect the neighbors, but in an apartment it is another matter. Also, the time of the meeting needs to consider neighbors, e.g. when the meeting ends late, guests need to leave without much noise.

Second there are very important issues when including minors in a gathering. Parental consent may be needed in some cases, e.g. when a child from another faith expresses a desire to visit or attend the meeting. Taking minors on trips can have important consequences in the case of an accident. The rule is to be aware and not create any opportunity for the enemy to enter into the picture.

It is also vital to use wisdom when ministering to people. Issues like male/female relationships are very important. When meeting with someone to counsel, it is vital to have more than one present to avoid any accusation of sexual abuse. In this the common sense never to meet alone with someone of the opposite sex is absolutely essential. It is best to do ministry within the midst of the body of believers gathered together and most issues can be dealt with in the body where it is open. This is also why it is good to have couples lead together. In terms of counseling it is also very important to choose one's words carefully. Counseling is not for everyone and there are strict guidelines from professional counselors regarding this profession. Often simple Biblical advice is to be preferred, but if this is called "counseling" it opens all kind of doors to litigation if something goes wrong. A very simple way to avoid problems is to avoid using the term "counseling" and simply offer to talk to someone and pray with them. Do not make any outrageous claims when you pray and offer advice, but rather let the results speak for themselves.

It is also very important to be cautious in the same way when praying for healing. Never tell someone to stop medication – let the person make the decision, preferably with a medical doctor's input. It is far better to have a surprised physician confirm a healing than to make such a claim and be shown to be wrong. This, more than anything else, has discredited the ministry of healing in the body of Christ. Make sure you know the facts before you make claims. Some time ago I was given a video to watch where a young lady experienced a miraculous healing and I have no doubt that she was healed of major problems. Unfortunately, her testimony included statements that she was coughing up portions of her liver – and medically that is impossible. This type of nonsensical testimony discredits the whole testimony and should be avoided. Simply pray for healing and let the fruit be shown in the lives being healed and restored. It brings glory to God and closes the door to the enemy to pursue legal action and discredit our testimony.

In terms of financial issues, make sure that proper books are kept and no money is misappropriated. If a decision is made to formally incorporate and to seek charitable status, legal advice is highly recommended. There are specific laws covering these matters and this is not the place to even try to cover the details. As networks develop, legal advice for the structures will be important, particularly if the network is set up to receive and manage funds for unregistered house churches. Personally, I look forward to the day when there is no charitable status, but for now we need to be aware of these matters and the laws pertaining to them.

There are no doubt more issues that we can discuss, but the key is to be aware of potential legal matters and seek the necessary input to make wise decisions and avoid legal traps.

Open the Door

This little booklet does not answer every question on house churches, nor will it or any other book for that matter. It was written simply to provide some practical guidelines for those who want to open the doors of their houses to invite others to meet Jesus and be the church. Ultimately it is not difficult to begin a house church. All you need is to seek the Lord and be willing to open the door and share your life with others. You don't need any man's permission to be obedient to the Lord. In fact, I cannot put it any better than that old fisherman called Peter when he wrote 2 Peter 1:3-11:

> *His divine power has given us everything*
> *we need for life and godliness through our*
> *knowledge of him who called us by his*
> *own glory and goodness. Through these he*
> *has given us his very great and precious*
> *promises, so that through them you may*
> *participate in the divine nature and escape*
> *the corruption in the world caused by evil*
> *desires.*

For this very reason, make every effort to add to your faith goodness; and to goodness, knowledge; and to knowledge, self-control; and to self-control, perseverance; and to perseverance, godliness; and to godliness, brotherly kindness; and to brotherly kindness, love. <u>For if you possess these qualities in increasing measure, they will keep you from being ineffective and unproductive in your knowledge of our Lord Jesus Christ.</u> But if anyone does not have them, he is nearsighted and blind, and has forgotten that he has been cleansed from his past sins.

Therefore, my brothers, be all the more eager to make your calling and election sure. For if you do these things, you will never fall, and you will receive a rich welcome into the eternal kingdom of our Lord and Savior Jesus Christ.

Did you hear that? You have everything you need to be effective and productive! Go ahead and open the door!

God bless,

Willie

APPENDIX

Through this booklet we have made reference to a number of resources that I have written as we embarked on this journey of faith. We recommend that you read the following if you have not done so before:

Restoring the broken foundations
This book was the first and addresses the foundational issues about the church and why the new wine will tear the old structures. It covers topics like the history of the church structures, fivefold ministry, the untapped resource of members' gifts, the models of Biblical leadership and sacred cows of Charismatic Christianity and the foundations of Covenant relationships.

Ordinary people extraordinary royal priests
This book followed as God led me on a journey through the letter to the Hebrews and the fact that in Christ the Levitical priesthood was replaced with the order of Melchizedek. Recognizing that the Western Church's structure is a semi-Christianized version of the Levitical model and replaced the New Testament model that

functioned since the early century, it cannot simply be changed to accommodate the new wine. We need a total new wineskin to allow the priesthood of the believer to function. This is a foundational book on the priesthood of the believer and a call to walk out of the comfort zones of unfruitful faith.

Radical Authenticity

This Book followed the first two in taking this vision to the practical realities of how to be the church and walk in The Way. It is a call to walk in The Way and to be the church – a call to be radically authentic.

Following this little booklet, I wrote a book on our journey out of the established church and the practical issues we faced as we adjusted to the realities of establishing house churches. This book, **"THE JOURNEY - Learning to walk in The Way"**, is in the process of being published. It will be a valuable resource for anyone making the transition.

Willie Joubert

About the Author

Dr. Willie Joubert was born in what was known as Tanganyika in East Africa and grew up on a farm that his parents pioneered after World War 2. It was an amazing childhood growing up in amidst wild animals with no hydro, phones, radios or TVs! When he was 11 they moved to a farm in South Africa. Going to school in the nearby town unbeknownst to him at the time was the fact that one of his classmates in Grade 6 would be his future wife. For those interested, Willie has also written a book covering the lives of his parents and it is available as eBook on Amazon – A Century on African Soil.

Following graduation, he attended the University of Pretoria where he completed a Master's degree in Semitic Languages and a degree in Theology and subsequently a Ph.D. in Old Testament Studies. Dr. Joubert taught Semitic Languages for 7 years at the University of Pretoria before he immigrated to Canada with his wife, Eda, and three children. In Canada he pastored in traditional churches as Presbyterian Minister and then in non-denominational settings, worked in church planting as well as in prayer ministry and applying his faith in business settings and in support of para-church ministries. These journeys led to a re-examining of the Biblical foundations of the Church and a conclusion that the future of the church will necessitate a return to the simplicity of the early church in small home-based churches where ordinary people will do the work of ministry.

With this conviction Willie and Eda pioneered a home church and began to network with others. In the process he wrote a number of books and shared the copies with friends and with anyone interested in these. Recently he decided to formally publish these books so that a wider audience can tap into the resources. This book is a practical Kingdom resource and how-to-book on establishing and leading house churches. May it be a catalyst to the birth of many churches!